Praise for The Women's Code
Book

"This book is compassionat ... r women who are overwork ... st, and who both have and are ... e for and from other women. Chelette is a positive and practical thinker."

Phyllis Chesler Ph.D, author of *Women and Madness, Woman's Inhumanity to Woman,* and *An American Bride in Kabul.*

"Beate Chelette has knocked the ball out of the park with this essential paradigm shifter for women of all ages and all walks of life. The Women's Code's *Happy Woman Happy World* will completely transform the way we relate to each other, to the men in our lives, and to our children and grandchildren. And this, in turn, will transform the entire consciousness of humanity!"

Dr. Marilyn Joyce, The Vitality Doctor™, author of *INSTANT E.N.E.R.G.Y.™*, creator of KickCancerInTheCan.com

"I really enjoyed Happy Woman Happy World. My only wish is that I had read this when I was in the crash and burn phase during my twenties and thirties! However, there are many relevant points for any age or career stage. It is a revolutionary concept for me to expect happiness at work. I am still thinking about how that can inform my career goals moving forward. Happiness really should be the goal for all parts of life. Love it."

Connie Dean, Director at Microsoft, married mother of two adult children

"If you are struggling, this gives you the tools to break apart the issues and manage them. If you are on a happy cycle, you are given the gift of permission to enjoy every moment. I found it to be a very positive process, and I have every intention of working back through some of the areas in which I need more personal development. Thank you, Beate!"

Eileen Lonergan, 47, owner of EileenLonergan.com website design, married mother of three

"Author Beate Chelette's *Happy Woman Happy World* joins the ranks of game-changing books such as Dale Carnegie's *How to Win Friends and Influence People*, Napoleon Hill's *Think and Grow Rich*, John Gray's *Men Are From Mars and Women Are From Venus*, and the best-selling titles of Anthony Robbins, such as *Awaken the Giant Within* and *Unlimited Power*.

Don't let the title fool you: *Happy Woman Happy World* speaks volumes to both sexes about finding your own rhythm in life, being true to who you are and where your priorities lie, and most importantly, the invaluable truth of living no one's life other than your own. Chelette's concept of the "ego-RHYTHM" will become part of the cultural lexicon for decades to come. Men and women alike don't want to miss this one."

Alex Simon, co-editor The Hollywood
Interview.com, blogger Huffington Post

"After reading *Happy Woman Happy World*, I felt validated. Beate explains the natural phases women go through and calls them ego-RHYTHMs. Understanding that I am in my Me ego-RHYTHM allowed me to shift my focus and put more energy toward personal growth. Soliciting encouragement from girlfriends can be a valuable tool in navigating life. The Core Code of Conduct is a solid model of how women can obtain harmony by supporting each other instead of working against each other. I will have my daughters read *Happy Woman Happy World* as I feel it is an exceptional tool to help them embrace each phase of their lives with peace and balance."

Christine Harris, 45-year-old stay at home mom,
mother to 2 daughters, married 20 years.

"I'm literally hypnotized by The Women's Code. I'm so relieved to know that I'm not deranged, selfish or a bad mother because I've decided to take the lead in my own life. Thank you, everything you say is so right."

Claire Blick, married stay at home mother
of three, and new entrepreneur

"I love the concept of the ego-RHYTHM. It makes sense that different things would be important to me at different times in my life, but I had never realized this until I read *Happy Woman Happy World*. I am in my career ego-RHYTHM now, so once I realized that I could focus primarily on my career, I felt like a weight was lifted off my shoulders. Of course I still focus some energy on my family, my health, my friendships and other areas of my life but those are going well and I really only need to make sure they continue to go well. My energy is primarily focused on building up my business and my client list and I start each day knowing I am doing the right thing at the right time."

Lisa Shalek, 46, freelance editor and homeschooling mother of four.

"As a business owner and single mom of three young daughters, I can't say enough about how *Happy Woman Happy World* has helped me to recognize there is a time and season for everything. I am inspired to stop and celebrate the time I am going through now and recognize which ego-RHYTHM I am currently in, be okay with it, and then embrace it fully, instead of constantly trying to do everything perfectly all the time. *Happy Woman Happy World* has shown me that true success comes through asking for support from others. It's okay to ask for and receive help. By working together instead of fighting against one another, constantly trying to do it all alone—women become 100 times more powerful. Thank you, Beate, for an incredible and defining book for all women."

Lacy Arnold, single mother of three, CEO/Founder LeanMoms.com

"Finally a book that is not just for women but also for their men. *Happy Woman Happy World* doesn't just illustrate or explain the difficult balancing act between career and family, it SIMPLIFIES the process of living it."

Reinhard Haas, 50, divorced, father of two, author and lifestyle writer

"Your book is phenomenal and I loved it! After reading *Happy Woman Happy World* I realized I am doing some things right. Although I'm still overwhelmed with many aspects of life, it was great to understand I'm not alone. I look forward to truly implementing (rather than conveniently living ego-RHYTHM only when my life is in turmoil) and learning to use it as an everyday tool for my life. I can't wait to create my "Want it All" list and begin to implement it with ego-RHYTHM in order to keep my life balanced and enjoy being human again. I look forward to continuing my journey with Happy Woman Happy World, my new life jacket."

Tanya Rivera, 38, career counselor for college students

"While reading *Happy Woman Happy World* I realized that that I'm not the only woman in the world who struggles with her day-to-day "helicopters." Now I know how to focus my energy on things which are really important for ME. I learned how to take time out for myself and how to not make myself available for everyone at any time. I know now that my life has different phases or rhythms – you just have to accept them. That makes it easier to handle my personal situation at the moment. Women shouldn't look at other women as "enemies," but rather help each other to reach our goals. Life could be so much easier without envy and competition. We just have to spread Beate's message! I love *Happy Woman Happy World* because Beate shared her own examples and experiences so I could relate and clearly understand what she means."

Jutta Kiesl, 47, owner of a language school and mother of two teenagers

"The Women's Code is unique in that it addresses all facets of a woman's life: family, career, personal, spiritual, leisure. It gently coaxed me to set priorities that allow me to be successful and healthy now. The smorgasbord of tools showed me how to trust my instincts, respect myself, and go forth and conquer while embracing the gifts and strengths of those around me!"

Karen D., single mom and entrepreneur

"When I picked up *Happy Woman Happy World* I did not know what to expect. Within pages I was reading about a former "she-tyrant" supervisor that I had. Suddenly, I realized her behavior had nothing to do with me. Moreover, learning about the "art of asking for support" was fabulous. This is a quick guide to understanding how to phrase a request to your boss, husband, significant other or just about anyone, so that you get what you want without generating resentment."

Paulina A., attorney

"Thank you for the unique concept and for the strength and intelligence you share. You are making a difference."

Phyllis Leslie, small business owner

"Every woman should learn about The Women's Code if they want to have a more fulfilled and successful life. My path is much clearer now."

Franny Armstrong, romance novel author

"Your blueprint for achieving goals is valuable because you're precise. But what endured long after is your intent to help women. That genuineness of pursuit has the power to influence at a distance."

Beverly Burwald, screenwriter

"Eye-opening! Enlightened me to new concepts and I look forward to getting all I want!"

Kathrin Alt, fine art photographer

"When I went through the exercise where I had to list my task-specific goals – my true self was revealed. Yes, I want to get ahead in my career and make more money. Who doesn't? However, I want to be a Marketing Director. So now, how do I do that specifically? What steps at my current company (since I like the industry) do I have to take in order to achieve this specific goal? These are questions that I need to focus on, instead of the generalization of 'make more money.' I now have a game plan in place."

Benja Stig Fagerland, business blogger

"I am hoping you can put on your big boot of confidence and kick out of me what is holding me back."

Carolyn Schirmacher, photographer

"You sound like a very untwisted sister!"

Kelly Valen, Author of *The Twisted Sisterhood*

THE WOMEN'S CODE®
PRESENTS

HAPPY WOMAN
HAPPY WORLD

The Foolproof Fix that Takes You from
Overwhelmed to Awesome!

BEATE CHELETTE

Happy Woman Happy World

Published in the United States by Visualist Publishing LLC
2801 Ocean Park Blvd., Suite 188
Santa Monica, CA 90405
Telephone: USA 310 452 4461
Email: info@VisualistPublishing.com
www.VisualistPublishing.com

Art Direction: Joseph Gilbert; *Cover Design:* Humblenations; *Layout & Design:* Rick Soldin

First Edition, 2013

ISBN 978-0-9889868-6-2

Names have been changed and recognizable characteristics disguised for all people in the book, except quoted experts, in order to protect their privacy. This book is not intended as a substitute for the medical advice of physicians. The reader should consult a physician in matters relating to his/her health and particularly with respect to any symptoms that may require diagnosis or medical attention.

Visualist Publishing books are available for purchase in bulk for educational, business, sales, or promotional purposes. For purchases contact: info@VisualistPublishing.com

In loving memory of my father,

who thought that all my ideas were great.

And to my daughter, Gina Sophia.

Of all the things I did, I did you best.

CONTENTS

ACKNOWLEDGEMENTS

*Nothing can dim the light
which shines from within.*

MAYA ANGELOU, *AUTHOR AND POET*

When I speak to audiences and tell them my story, I am always amazed that my life worked out the way it did. While I am a woman who wants it all and can't take no for an answer, there are many people along the way who helped to get me to get to where I am.

My daughter Gina Sophia Chelette is The ONE. Without her I would not have had the reason, or the drive, to get up every day to do it all over again. Kelly deLaat and Carol Courneya are the two women responsible for restoring my faith in womankind. Without you, ladies, I would have given up hope a long time ago. Great thanks goes to my team, the people behind the scenes that keep things running: Michael Albany, Nancy Eubanks, Mary Fischer, Jennie Jorgens, Alina Morosan, Sol Orena, Lisa Shalek, and Christine Rivera.

Thanks also go to my family in Germany who, in their own unique way, contributed to this book. To my friends, business partners, and stalwart supporters, who patiently let me helicopter away into yet even more new ideas–you always just seem to know how to get me back safely to planet reality. You guys are awesome and I thank you for that: Michael Drew, Joseph Gilbert, Michael Grecco, Reinhard Haas, Andrea Reindl, Tim Smith, and The Wizard, Roy Williams.

Most importantly, I want to thank the women who so graciously and with unwavering enthusiasm believed in me and The Women's Code. I never thought I would say this, but I cherish you and your compassion, stubbornness, individuality, strength, and your great friendship: Ruta Fox, Anne Windsor, Ninaya Strandberg, Annett Sachs, Dr. Marilyn Joyce, Alice Marie De Prisco, Dorit Thies, Victoria Hulett Gross, and Dagmar Schmid.

I want to acknowledge each and every woman and man who had a part in or an opinion on the creation of The Women's Code. You know who you are.

Finally, my eternal gratitude and thanks go to Bill Gates for changing my life.

"What's the point of making it to the top if you end up alone? Success means nothing if you have no one to share it with."

BEATE CHELETTE

WHAT WOMEN WANT

When it comes to the enormous challenge of our time—to systematically and relentlessly pursue more economic opportunity in our lands—we don't have a person to waste and we certainly don't have a gender to waste.

HILLARY RODHAM CLINTON, 67TH U.S. SECRETARY OF STATE

The Women's Code has the power to redefine who we are, what we are, and what we want. Truly, modern women want it all. And with The Women's Code, we can have it, we just need to learn how.

This is your story. The story about wanting, in its simplest terms, a fulfilled and happy life.

It's about wanting a job that gratifies us—where we are seen and heard whether or not we choose a high-powered career or move ahead at a more modest pace.

We definitely want that special relationship at home that allows us to be who we truly are. Where we have a place to go to that is safe and puts our soul at ease. We want a partner to have meaningful conversations with about things that matter to us.

We want real friendships that are based on mutual trust and respect with true interaction. We want to be accepted and able to expose our insecurities and vulnerabilities without the fear of gossip or backstabbing.

We want the freedom to change the rules when the old ones don't serve us anymore.

The Women's Code is your foolproof fix to the chaos and dissatisfaction in your life. It is the final piece of the puzzle, where everything you have been trying to make fit, finally falls into place. This is your chance to discover who you really are underneath all your responsibilities, obligations, restrictions, and rules, without judgment. And most importantly, this is where you learn that your deepest fear of not being enough isn't true.

I know things about you that you don't know yet. I see amazing gems in you which have been buried that The Women's Code is going to unearth. I know with absolute certainty that you are capable of doing incredible things. I speak from experience because just like so many of you, I once was fearful, constantly searching, and never really happy. That was the pressure that pushed me to create The Women's Code.

What makes me an expert on all this? My reputation as a successful entrepreneur and self-made millionaire has made me a sought after public speaker and career consultant. In 2006, I sold my photography business to a company that Bill Gates owned and I made millions.

My passion and expertise lie in showing women how to become more successful in their careers and live lives that are in harmony and balance.

But did I retire? No way! I think it's in my DNA to always be busy. But now, unlike my tortured past, I know how to avoid becoming overwhelmed by all the demands in my life and I've finally discovered time to have good friends and just enjoy life.

That wasn't always the case, I assure you. I have known great struggle and hardship in my life. There were times during what I call my decade of disaster when I wasn't sure where my three-year-old daughter and I would live or how I was going to pay the bills. I've known scary times when no one, not a single friend or relative, was there to help. One day my once-successful photography production business went under, and I lost all my clients—and billings of half a million dollars—in a matter of 24 hours, right after the tragic events of 9/11. The stress got so bad that I developed serious physical problems and there were times I wasn't sure I was going to make it, yet through it all, I had perseverance and the determination to share my brilliant idea for The Women's Code.

I carried the belief that somehow things wouldn't always be *this hard* and I would, one day, be able to turn my life around. Now you can learn in this book what took me over thirteen years to figure out the hard way.

Unlike other programs, The Women's Code addresses all phases of your life. It unlocks the knowledge that got buried along the way and allows you through awareness, support and collaboration to turn the seemingly impossible complexity of who you are into clarity and focus to create a happier life. You can do it. I know you can. And most importantly, you deserve it.

Already, The Women's Code has given thousands of women the answers we need to live a life with connection, purpose, and passion. It enables us to discover how to seamlessly weave together all the various parts of our lives such as career, family, personal interests and more. All the different aspects of our lives can be balanced and working together, instead of coming at us from different angles and working against each other. Work no longer has to conflict with family and children. And personal pursuits no longer have to cost us romance.

Certainly, The Women's Code has been a long time in the making and I have a lot of thank you cards to send to our brave foremother iconoclasts who did everything in their power to break through restrictive norms and stereotypes. They changed history and the world's perceptions about who women truly are and what a woman can accomplish. The Women's Code honors those who stood up first and made everything, even this book, possible. We know who you are and your contributions will be remembered.

Now, it's time for our next evolution. Thankfully, progress never stops. We are in a continual process of polishing the diamond to let its beauty shine through. What you are about to learn is the key to getting everything you have always wanted.

Are you ready to learn what you always knew in your heart you needed?

It's time.

Start now.

You'll learn about: ego-RHYTHM, the transformational time-based concept showing you the natural way to let things flow; the Women's Core Code of Conduct, which shows us a way to live without devastating our own or other women's self-confidence; how to establish a functioning Work-Life Balance with the help of a few easy tools; and the Three Pillars of Awareness, Support and Collaboration that help you move forward. These are easy ways to make not only your work life, but your home life so much easier.

Don't wait to turn the page.

In this book. And in your life.

WOMEN'S PURSUIT
OF HAPPINESS

*A woman with a voice is by definition a
strong woman. But the search to find that
voice can be remarkably difficult.*

MELINDA GATES, *PHILANTHROPIST*

This is our decade. The Decade of Empowered Women. Women
are stepping up into serious power worldwide and taking charge
of making our lives happen. The choices are ours. Today we can
literally be and do anything we want.

Feminism inspired women to don pantsuits and climb the ranks
in the working world. We did this because we believed we
were missing something at home. Homemaking, child rearing,
and making our husbands happy gradually lost their appeal.
Women wanted more. We wanted to contribute our ideas and be
challenged intellectually.

But when it came to equal opportunity and equal pay, women
found that entering the workforce was a challenge. We dug deeper
for the strength to enter uncharted waters in search of fulfillment,
wholeheartedly believing that our careers would lead us there. We
became breadwinners and bosses.

This demonstrates how powerful women are when we put our mind to something. In fact, Time magazine reports that young women are out-earning men in urban areas in comparable jobs at a rate between 8% to 20%[1] and Dēmos, a non-partisan public policy research and advocacy organization, reports that "Young women are now much more likely to have at least a bachelor's degree—a complete reversal of the gender gap from 1980. In 2000, 31 percent of young women had at least a bachelor's compared to 28 percent of young men. In 2011, 37 percent of young women had at least a bachelor's degree compared to 29 percent of young men[2]." That's a huge accomplishment for women. We went from significantly under-earning to out-earning men and are graduating from higher educational institutions in record numbers in just 50 years!

The scales are tipping internationally as well. *The Third Billion Report* published by Booz & Company[3] states, "Nearly 1 billion women around the world could enter the global economy during the coming decade. They are poised to play a significant role in countries around the world." And the famed Shriver Report *A Woman's Nation Changes Everything*[4] says, "We are in the midst of a fundamental transformation of the way America works and lives."

Women are taking charge. We are becoming leaders and the world is taking notice. Well, hooray! This is good, right? After all, feminists risked everything by taking women's liberation to the streets and to the workplace. They fought hard, hammering through the glass ceiling. When necessary, the courtroom became their battleground. Our feminist foremothers succeeded so that we could reach even greater heights. Certainly, we achieved gender equality in many important areas. While the numbers may not be equal in political or corporate leadership, we are well on our way. Thousands of doors that were previously closed have been opened. One would think that women would be happier than ever before. After all, we are buying our own houses and diamonds, and we are celebrating our success with expensive champagne.

Women are happy because we got what we wanted. Right? And most importantly because it has been such a battle to get to the top, women are supporting other women along the way. Right?

Unfortunately, both statements are VERY wrong.

Indeed, this is the Decade of Empowered Women. But is it also the Decade of Empowered Happy Women? Overall, statistics report a devastating answer. No.

The state of women today isn't quite the happy ending we had envisioned. Indeed, women have more opportunities than ever to become whatever we choose to be and create whatever lives we want. But here's the truth that backfired on us—statistically, women are *more* depressed, *more* clinically stressed, *more* anxious, *more* troubled and lonelier than ever before. Sadly women today express that they are experiencing the opposite of fulfillment. The Shriver report stated women feel "isolated, invisible, stressed, and misunderstood."

Shocking, I know. Once my head stopped spinning, I wanted to know why. How did our dream of independence and influence become our new nightmare? After heavy research, feedback from private clients and the thousands who attend my workshops, plus five decades of my own painful personal experiences banging my head against this very problem, I found the answer.

The answer is two-fold.

Basically, there just was no tried and true road map. There are no clear examples and no successful women who have gone before us to share the critical information on how to succeed. As women rose through the ranks, we had to figure out how to get ahead alone, making it up as we went along.

Secondly, there were very few women's networks to turn to. Women's private clubs where female members helped each other connect, mentor, or coach each other on their new roles in the workplace were few and far between.

In comparison, men have had this kind of support for generations. For every career a man aspires to achieve there are an abundance of role models, mentorships, documents, road maps, fraternities, and private networks to help them get ahead. The connections in "The Old Boys Network" made a man's career advancement a breeze compared to women trying to get ahead in the workplace. Women were left to fend for themselves. Certainly, we became stronger for it but not necessarily happier.

What is the source of our discontent? Why all this unhappiness, stress, and depression in the workplace? It's not that we aren't educated. We are. It's not that women don't have the chops to succeed. We do. We've proven that we've got the goods. What, then, is the underlying issue that affects millions of women? Sadly, it's not what you think, the problem is less "out there" than previously assumed.

What are women experiencing at the office that is the root cause of our discontent at and with work?

More and more women lament that joining the workforce simply added another shift to our day because, for the majority of us, our household duties didn't lighten up. It's not like women exchanged one job for another. Oh no. Women added an extra helping of responsibility to our plates in the name of fulfillment. And now we find ourselves doing double duty in a 24/7 lifestyle that doesn't stop. For so many women, we get home from work only to find another job waiting for us. Laundry. Dinner. Mother. Wife. Community. Every one of them demanding our full attention. When do we sleep? When do we get to relax and actually enjoy all the benefits of being successful when all we do is work at the office and then work again at home?

But then women haven't found the office to be as rosy as we thought it would be, either. The issue isn't always with men who throw roadblocks in our path, often the issue is with other women who feel threatened. The friction comes from women who are so afraid to lose all that we worked so hard for that we don't welcome and mentor the next generation of talented women entering the workforce. It saddens me greatly to say that these women actually block progress by making it more difficult for women to rise through the ranks to substantial positions and paychecks.

Meredith Bryan, in her *Marie Claire* article "The Pink Ceiling"[5] asks the question, "Why do ambitious young women say they hate working for other women?" She goes on to quote studies that say (and I'm paraphrasing here) that today women prefer working for men because there is less hostility. *Hostility*. The article then asks if "equal opportunity helped make us our own worst enemies." *Enemies*. And by *us*—the author means other women. Why did we work so hard to achieve so much only to squabble amongst ourselves and bully each other?

I believe it's because women are scared of losing what we sacrificed everything to get. For women, especially in the beginning, it was like the Wild West at the office. No rules, no codes, and no guidelines on how to get ahead.

Statistics don't forecast sun and happiness in our future either. Forty-five percent of workers said they have been bullied at work, according to a new study just released by CareerBuilder.com[6]. Let's break it down into real numbers. In an office with 50 employees, 22 are bullied. Of those 22, a staggering 18 will leave their jobs.

Corporate America is realizing that bullies are too expensive to keep on the payroll. According to WorkDoctor.com,[7] the estimated potential annual cost to an average Fortune 500 Company in lost productivity from bullying is more than $8,000,000. Not to mention lost revenues from turnover, litigation, settlements, and disability. The losses are staggering and are in the tens of millions. It hurts me to write this but female-to-female bullying has been reported at a rate of 80%. *Eighty percent.* New phrases have been coined such as "She-Tyrant" and "Queen Bee" to describe power hungry women at the top who terrorize their colleagues and co-workers.

According to Dr. Gary Namie of the Workplace Bullying Institute[8], "Workplace bullying leads to employee stress that can impact workplace productivity, quality of work, and have negative financial impact on the victim. In a survey conducted in 2013, 15 percent of those bullied in the workplace left work early on disability or took an early retirement; 18 percent used a combination of short-term disability, long-term disability or both; and nearly 10 percent used unpaid Family Medical Leave Act (FMLA) time because of stress-related concerns."

Indeed, the problem isn't "out there." It has grown from within our own gender. I'm sure that our foremother's dreams of liberation didn't include women treating our sisters so horribly in the office. How did women become this way and how can women tolerate how other successful women are being portrayed publicly?

When women like Hilary Clinton, Sarah Palin, Carly Fiorina and Meg Whitman went after what they wanted on their way to the top, many media outlets publically ripped them to shreds. From pointing out their physical flaws to criticizing their wardrobes and judging their hair color, the chatter was sidetracked with unimportant issues that took the focus away from a trailblazer getting the credit she deserved for advancing into a position of great leadership. How can we allow this to happen?

Perhaps, if we had had some mentorship, it wouldn't be like this. For example, most women don't train their successors because we are not even aware that this is a necessary aspect of moving up. We weren't trained. So how would we know how to train others? Too often, women get stuck in middle management because we don't know how mutually beneficial it is to mentor those below us. As we mentor those below us to advance, we are mentored from above to advance into our boss's position as well. That is how one moves up in corporate culture.

For example, as soon as men are hired, they take a look at the corporate ladder. They expect to eventually take their bosses job, because they assume that their boss will move up as well, it's expected of them. And their boss knows it. No one can advance without a competent successor plan in place. A UK survey[9] of 3,000 members of the Institute of Leadership and Management shows that two thirds of the men expected to become a manager. But only half of the women did. Women held onto their positions so tightly that we didn't look up and see the next opportunity that could be ours. This created tension, stress, and toxicity that have overflowed into all aspects of women's lives, not just the workplace.

One of the first women to identify this was Phyllis Chesler[10] with her groundbreaking book *"Woman's Inhumanity to Woman,"* published in 2001 and reissued in 2009. She writes, "Yes, many women swear by their female friends and relatives with whom they live, socialize, work, pray, and with whom they do political or religious work. Most women have several best friends, whose support they value deeply. I certainly do. As so many women say, "I would be lost without my close female friends ... However, we also live in a world in which second wives assist their new husbands in custody battles designed to destroy a first wife, both economically and custodially; a world in which best girlfriends and female colleagues sometimes steal their friends' husbands, female partners, social networks, or jobs—and in such a way that the original woman is "disappeared" from her former life; a world in which some female judges and female physicians value male plaintiffs and male patients over their female counterpart; a world in which many female jurors do not believe female rape and battery victims; a world in which many female employers prefer their male employees; and one in which the same female employees who put up with the most arrogant and bullying of male bosses are much harder on their female bosses, whom they resent and often sabotage."

In 2009, Betsey Stevenson and Justin Wolfers penned the famous report *The Paradox of Declining Female Happiness*[11] which states, "The lives of women in the United States have improved over the past 35 years by many objective measures, yet we show that measures of subjective well-being indicate that women's happiness has declined both absolutely and relative to men."

So what was our prize for entering the workforce and liberating ourselves? A decline in happiness.

That just doesn't feel right, nor should it. The good news is now that we are aware of the problem, we can change it in the same way women did with inequality. To find both satisfaction and fulfillment in our careers we need a new shift in our thinking. That's what The Women's Code is all about. It's a revolutionary system of new concepts, principles, tools, and strategies that work for women today both at work and in our personal relationships.

The Women's Code is a light in the darkness. It shines a spotlight on what we need to do next. It raises our awareness. It teaches us how to ask for and receive the support we need to be successful and happy. It gives us a framework for how to have fulfilling and productive collaborations at work, at home, and in our spare time. Yes, I said spare time. When you follow the principles of The Women's Code you can actually create more time in your day to do what you love and have time to be with whom you love.

THE WOMEN'S CODE TIP

Women often just keep going, going, going until we crash and burn. Let's not wait until we get sick, fired, or divorced before we finally learn to lean on each other in a way that creates inner confidence and trust within our own gender to enliven us.

With The Women's Code, women can be successful and lead well because we feel connected and understood. When we feel understood, we feel like we have a voice and feel confident using it to speak out about what is meaningful to us. I can relate to this because for many years I felt misunderstood.

My journey began when I was still living month-to-month and it came to a tipping point when I ran a division of a large company. What I learned from working for myself and as a corporate employee changed me forever. Of all the people who taught me so many valuable lessons, it's Sandy who I will never forget. She had worked for over a decade at the company I was brought in to run and she knew how to play the corporate game. Year after year, Sandy gained a little bit more power in title and salary. At first, when I was the newcomer, we seemed to get along quite well. We attended the same meetings and worked on a few projects together.

After working with her for a while, Sandy began to allude to information and important company directives that only she knew. She hinted about contractual details that were "reserved" for only a few select executives. She presented herself as knowing company secrets that others didn't. It seemed odd to me that a prolific and successful company would not share its vision with its employees. But I was new. So, for the moment, I didn't think much of it.

Things got toxic when the CEO promoted me to be Sandy's boss. She began campaigning against me behind my back. Conversations abruptly stopped when I walked into an office where a group of team members were talking. Doors closed for telephone conversations. And an atmosphere of distrust and secrecy was ever present. It was the complete opposite of collaboration.

I discovered quickly that there were indeed no secrets. Sandy was playing a game that she designed to make people think she was in power and important. At one point she challenged me outright. Sandy said to my face that she had survived all kinds of bosses and that she would survive me, too. That is how confident she was about her power play.

I didn't know what to do. This certainly wasn't what I had signed up for when I accepted the position. So, I fell back onto my usual defenses. I pretended that I didn't need camaraderie in the workplace. But without it, I was miserable and lonely. Why didn't she communicate? If there were issues, why didn't she privately confer with me? We could have worked it out. I felt so betrayed. I enjoyed the job but not the relationships with my own team. I wonder to this day if this type of behavior was actually encouraged from the top down? Corporate made it my personal problem and said that I didn't know how to lead. I didn't get much support.

Finally, I wasn't living month-to-month anymore. In fact, there were more zeros in my compensation than ever, but I wasn't happy. I felt alone. I didn't feel understood or heard. I tried to convince myself that I could do this and make myself fit in. I tried to convince myself that it would get better. But it didn't.

My intention was to push the women on my team to step up and become effective, respected, and fearless leaders. But I experienced roadblock after roadblock. In fact, my team had the opposite of collaboration. These women withheld critical information that made it impossible for the team to get their jobs done on time. They thought that withholding information protected their positions. (In the end, they were SO wrong.)

I was at the top, higher up than I ever had been. There was no one guiding me. I was figuring it out myself, mistake by mistake, how to effectively manage and lead my global team of thirty. The company didn't support a mentorship program, nor did they offer any solutions to my challenges. As unhappy as I was, if I hadn't gone through this, I might never have known just how bad things really were for women in corporate America.

Without support and guidance, I was in over my head and my confidence was sorely lacking. I was the boss, but I didn't own my leadership. If I had known about the principles of The Women's Code at the time, I would have been aware that women, like Sandy, were behaving like this simply because they were afraid of losing their jobs. From this awareness, I could have supported them by giving them the tools and reassurance they needed to get their job done. And I might have felt secure enough to ask for their support in return. Things could have been so different. We could have formed successful and powerful collaborations that supported all of our futures.

The Women's Code shows us how to ask for help and get the support we need and deserve. The truth is that support and confidence lead to happiness and success. Now I understand that the women who sabotaged me just wanted to be heard. They wanted their contributions to be acknowledged. They wanted their work to be respected. Unfortunately, we weren't communicating on that level so we couldn't find any common ground.

When women work together using The Women's Code, it is no longer so lonely or dangerous at the top. Women are liberated to lead and be powerful. Instead of terrorizing employees solely because we are the "boss" and can get away with it, The Women's Code teaches us how to become truly confident and lead with compassion.

The Women's Code isn't just for Baby Boomers or Generation X. Oh no. The next up-and-coming generation of young, talented women entering the workforce by the tens of millions need our help. They are called The Millennials and these young women are struggling with their careers and lifestyle. They have just gotten started in the work force but studies show that The Millennials suffer from a higher rate of stress than Boomers. Without finding the support and mentorship they need from other women, these problems will compound.

What I have found is that getting to the top doesn't guarantee we'll be happy. It simply means we bring all our baggage with us up through the ranks. When we arrive, we are still dealing with the same issues, only now they are compounded with greater stress and responsibility. The Women's Code can help. It can turn our guilt, perfectionism, sacrifice, isolation, dissatisfaction, and the struggle to fit in into clarity, confidence, ease, balance, and most importantly, fun.

THE TRIPLE PARADOX

I am sick and tired of being sick and tired.

FANNIE LOU HAMER, *CIVIL RIGHTS ACTIVIST*

Women are faced with a triple threat of paradoxes. A paradox is something that can't be accomplished because it contradicts itself. The Women's Code has identified three different paradoxes: the Female Success Paradox, the Goal Paradox, and the Superhuman Paradox.

The Female Success Paradox

During the Women's Liberation Movement, we looked beyond our lives at home. We asked ourselves, what would make us feel more fulfilled and happier. It quickly became clear that we wanted equality with men. So, we went after it. Equal pay. Equal access. Equal opportunities. Equal rights. We wanted to educate ourselves, and we wanted the option to keep our own last name after marriage.

This Female Success Paradox promised us that equality would bring happiness:

> Women said we wanted equality.
> Women thought equality would make us happy.
> Women got equality.
> Women aren't happier.

The path to attain equality was hard, but we stayed the course because there was something better and more worthwhile at the end of our quest for equal rights. Women were no longer content to only stay at home and raise a family. We wanted to get out there, explore, and compete. We wanted more in all areas of self-fulfillment. So, we set sail for an exciting, unknown destination.

This innate feeling of wanting more is something I can relate to. Perhaps you want more in your life, too? I was never content with what was available to me when I was growing up. I knew deep inside that there had to be more *out there.* An inexplicable longing for *something else* ran deep in my veins. My life was too restrictive, too small, there were too many constraints. But if anyone asked me specifically what I was seeking, I couldn't answer them. It was simply *not this.* It was *something else.*

What I did know is that I wanted to be successful and independent. I didn't care what that looked like. This comment mirrors precisely what I hear from many of my private coaching clients. Women want to achieve success in order to be in charge of our lives and make our own decisions. That is what "getting there" means for many women.

But here is our first dilemma. How can you "get there" if you don't know what "there" looks like?

I learned the hard way that there is no getting "there". Once we achieve what we think will make us happy, we discover something else that we want and we need to set sail again. The point I'm making here is that life is more difficult when we can't clearly define what we want to achieve. Without knowing our exact destination, how can we ever arrive? Or even know when we do?

When we don't know where we are going, it's difficult to experience a sense of happiness along the way. We feel lost looking for something that is vague and undefined. We feel that we are lacking something but we don't know quite what it is. Because we don't know what we want, we look around at others and begin to want what they have. *The grass always looks greener on the other side.* We do this because we are unclear or unable to define what we want. We want what others have because it looks good from the outside. The Women's Code changes this by showing you in Chapter 8 how to define what it is that you want.

The Goal Paradox

The Goal Paradox misleads us to think that the more we know, have, do, and achieve, the happier we will be. This paradox makes us believe that happiness is in the attainment of the goal. We fall into the trap of thinking if only we could buy the new car, get that promotion, or get engaged, then suddenly our lives would be complete and better than before. But when we do get that new car we realize it really is just a car and it didn't really make us happy. Whatever baggage we had in the trunk of the old one comes with us.

Attaining more and wanting something else is a never-ending process. We challenged ourselves and excelled. Whether it was at work or at home, we poured ourselves into everything with abandon. We thought by piling up more activities, that might make us happier. If we don't enjoy the process that leads up to the achievement, then we are unhappy all the way there.

So ... now what? If we achieved our goals and got what we thought would bring us happiness—and we're still not happy, what, then, is the solution? Arthur Ashe says it perfectly, "Success is a journey, not a destination. The doing is often more important than the outcome."

The Superhuman Paradox

Women were expected to excel in all areas of our lives without being given more time in the day to do it. Rather than being able to excel in a few areas, now women had to be superwomen. We were expected to be a great home decorator, and an amazing boss, and a loving mother, and a devoted wife. The list goes on and on. What's worse is that women are expected to do all this at once and achieve 100% success in everything. *Everything.*

Today, women are held to superhuman standards. The common assumption in our culture is that women who are successful in their careers are also great at everything else we do. Our homes look like a Martha Stewart magazine cover shoot, we've had kids but look like Heidi Klum (who had 4 children and wears a size 2) and we can cook up a fantastic gourmet meal to rival chef Gordon Ramsey. And women are supposed to do all this with a wink and a smile like it's all so effortless.

All women across the board, whether we work or not, are faced with a set of paradoxes. We are expected to excel in our career (or at least feel guilty if we don't,) while being the primary caregivers at home, plus take care of a multitude of other time consuming tasks like volunteering and gardening. And all the while, look our very best.

Actress and producer Sarah Jessica Parker said in an interview, "I think women of a certain generation, mine in particular, feel like we can have it all because that's what we were fed. It's like, we reap the benefits of the feminist movement—they did all the legwork and now we're going to try to be parents *and* successful business people *and* great wives *and* good friends *and* take a cooking class and blah, blah, blah..."

On the single mother front, reconciling the Superhuman Paradox is even more difficult. In 2012, there were 10.3 million single mothers living with children under 18. This statistic is up from 3.4 million in 1970[12]. For me this wasn't just a number, it was my life. As a single mother, I lived this story and felt the Superhuman Paradox all too well. Every day, I had to do everything by myself without anyone helping me out. Motherhood is a 24/7 job that never stops and can push single mothers to the brink of our emotional, physical, and financial limits. Still, the expectations are the same–achieve everything. At once. And with ease.

As I was assembling the puzzle pieces of The Women's Code, some concepts emerged with more clarity. Suddenly, it dawned on me. Was it possible that our internal and external struggles to achieve happiness caused the rift within our own gender? Do we seek out other women's weaknesses and tear them down so they don't appear to be better or more perfect than we are? I believe so.

If we're suffering from our own and society's expectations to be perfect in all areas of our lives at once, then would we subconsciously envy women we think have more of what we want? I think so.

Sure these "perfect" women may look like they have it together. They may look like they have the perfect life with the house, car, adoring husband, career, and still time to have time to actually bake cookies for their kid's birthdays. In reality, they may have only figured out how to do a few things successfully just like us.

Yet we find ourselves wanting what they have because we feel we are not enough the way we are. Does our insecurity become a source of rage against those who we feel have more of what we want? I think so.

This is precisely the very reason why I created ego-RHYTHM, a transformational time-based concept. It is time to stop this insanity. ego-RHYTHM does exactly that. It nullifies the unrealistic expectation that you have to do it all, all at once. More on ego-RHYTHM in the next chapter.

When we don't succeed at something expected of us, and even more importantly when we fail at delivering on our own expectations of ourselves, we often feel like absolute failures. For a woman's wellbeing, it's important to understand that being a successful woman (or a woman who wants it all) does not mean she must be someone who does it all at once. Or necessarily does everything equally well.

I am talking about real women like you and me. We are strong women with our own beliefs. We work too damn hard and strive for quality in our lives. Yet, we are often overwhelmed by relentless perfectionism. We need to confront these false expectations of being able to do everything all at once and being perfect in all areas of our lives. We begin confronting these expectations within ourselves, then at home, and then in the workplace. We need to address all areas of our lives. Otherwise, if we feel that even one area of our lives isn't perfect, it will chip away at our self-esteem and bring us down.

Amongst the thousands of women who have taken my live workshops or who I coach privately, rarely do I find someone who feels like she has it all together. I have met very few women who can confidently acknowledge her strengths and shortcomings with a sense of humor. Sheryl Sandberg, in her book *Lean In*[13], confessed that even though she was part of a circle of high-powered women, she felt fraudulent. She says, "Internal obstacles are rarely discussed and often underplayed. Throughout my life, I was told over and over about inequalities in the workplace and how hard it would be to have a career and family. I rarely heard anything, however, about the ways I might hold myself back. These internal obstacles deserve a lot more attention."

Indeed, the real struggle is within us. Because most of our struggles are the ones we put upon ourselves, we must first work within ourselves. We also need to strengthen ourselves because with success can also come great criticism. It's in our best interest to learn how to separate the naysayers from those who we should actually listen to. For example, British pop star Adele was slammed by some of her fans when she didn't drop all her maternity weight before she returned to the stage.

And personally, a former boyfriend was at my house relaxing and reading a magazine one evening when he pointed to a fashion model on a page and said: "This is what you used to look like." Well, thanks. For nothing. I couldn't believe it. Mind you, I was on serious medication to heal a digestive disorder. Still I was a very healthy weight and a size 6. But suddenly, I felt I had to justify to him why I wasn't 120 pounds anymore!

The funny thing is that his comment didn't seem at all hypocritical to him. He had bought into the cultural bias that says it's okay for men to bald and gain a gut but women must maintain our youthful figure as we age. The Superhuman Paradox strikes again. Women are expected to look younger, trimmer, and better even as we get older and work like crazy to achieve a career all while being great moms!

It saddens me to say this but a woman's looks count for a lot in the office. This is what people expect as you climb the corporate ladder as said by Lois P. Frankel, author of *Nice Girls Don't Get The Corner Office*[14]: "Competence is only table stakes. It's what gets you in the door. It's expected that you'll be competent, but competence alone won't move you forward. Research showed that about 55 percent of your credibility comes from how you look. How you sound accounts for an additional 38 percent. Only 7 percent of your credibility is based on what you say. If you don't look the part, you won't be recognized as a competent professional—no matter how smart or educated you are."

The Female Success Paradox that more professional success doesn't equate more happiness is just the beginning. Here are

THE WOMEN'S CODE TIP

No woman, no matter how talented or beautiful she is, can ever realistically hope to meet the demands and expectations placed on her by outside forces. We need to focus less on what we are expected to do, say, or weigh, and put more value on our individual and interpersonal attributes.

more examples of Superhuman Paradoxes that women fall prey to. Perhaps some are all too familiar? Take a look:

- ❋ Give birth, then breastfeed for at least six months, while you get back into shape in six-weeks, and are ready to resume your career

- ❋ Talk baby talk to the kids all day. And by night you transform into a dazzling dinner party conversationalist.

- ❋ Your husband desires a conservative PTA mom but expects you to be uninhibited in the bedroom.

- ❋ You're supposed to be impeccably groomed and fashionable at all times: at work, while grocery shopping, and schlepping kids from activity to activity.

- ❋ You're a fabulous girl on the go with a great social life yet still find time to devote yourself to caring for your elderly parents.

- ❋ You are expected to bake award-winning cupcakes and negotiate the $1 billion merger with ease.

- ❋ You can bend time and be in two places at once. Sure, you can put in the overtime required to make partner and pick up the kids by 5 p.m. from daycare.

- ❋ You are going to build a business with no start-up cash but you're expected to be all smiles and fun, never stressed out.

- ❋ Oh, and don't forget … pursue the corner office, lead your team, and serve an organic homemade dinner by 6 p.m.

Exhausted just reading this? I thought so! The Superhuman Paradox has destroyed our self-esteem and our ability to be happy. But remember, it's not true.

We don't have to live our lives by other's rules anymore. The Women's Code shows you how to achieve happiness and go after the success and relationships you desire by leveraging the natural flow and rhythm of our lives.

THE EGO-RHYTHM ANSWER TO HAVING IT ALL

Timing is the key to having it all.

BEATE CHELETTE, *ENTREPRENEUR AND AUTHOR*

Women today want it all. We worked too long and too hard not to get everything our hearts desire. But in the pursuit of our dreams we fell into the trap of thinking that we had to do it all at once. We had to pursue a career, have a family, learn to paint, travel, exercise, and more all at the same time. If we didn't, we felt like we were failing at the superimposed and unrealistic standards that somewhere along the way we bought into.

But these standards are simply crazy making. Dare I say, not humanly possible. Although when we were expected to do more (like work outside and inside the home) we weren't given more time in the day to get it done. While I fell into trying to do it all at the same time in my own life, a voice deep inside told me that there had to be a better way. It became my quest to figure this out. I just didn't believe that life was supposed to be so stressful.

Perhaps it's because I was born in Germany, where we're brought up to be methodical. Or maybe it's just my way of organizing myself, but I've always solved challenges by breaking them down into tangible and achievable goals, then they don't seem so far way. What I want feels possible and within my reach.

What I've discovered that I'm sharing with you here is a way for women to truly have it all. Seriously. It's possible. It just takes a little reworking of how we think we'll get it. I explain it like this: Imagine that your life is a loaf of bread and that you can slice it into different pieces. Some slices come out a little thicker and others a little thinner. Regardless, you wouldn't try to put the whole loaf of bread into your mouth to eat it all at once, right? Wouldn't you enjoy and savor it more slice by slice?

We can apply this analogy to our lives. Now, the question of "can we have it all" is a resounding yes. You can, but not by trying to do everything at once. Just like the example of putting a whole loaf of bread in your mouth. Impossible.

Rather, you divide your life into manageable slices that you can enjoy each, one by one while still getting to do it all. Certainly, what you want is going to be different from every other woman. It's so important to realize that we don't have to do everything the same as everyone else, or even want the same things at the same time. We can follow our individual desires that are unique to us. In all my years of leading workshops and private coaching, I have never ever heard two women who want the exact same thing.

Another important note is that there is a high probability that we will never be able to get everything done and completed, anyway! It is human nature once we accomplish one goal to naturally gravitate toward a new one. There isn't an end where we say, "Whew. I'm done. Now, I can just relax for the rest of my life."

Women are inspired beings. There will always be something around the horizon that is a new challenge. It's natural. It's life. When we embrace this notion, we can naturally flow from one phase of our life into the next where we will find, accomplish, or achieve something new—we can then let go of the stress and worry over not doing everything at once. No phase of our lives is forever. One will end and another will become our new main focus. This is a natural rhythmical movement of life that I call our ego-RHYTHM®[15].

> **ego-RHYTHM is an event or occurrence that takes place over a period of time, usually three to four years. It is a major, life-changing influence that determines your Main Focus.**

The first time I truly understood the ego-RHYTHM concept was when my daughter, Gina, was three years old. She had a terrible chest cold and was coughing at night, often all throughout the night. This went on for weeks. One evening, when the coughing was particularly bad, I kept checking on her constantly. Finally, I gave into my intuition that told me to grab her from her room and let her sleep in my bed. While I was getting ready for bed, I heard a sound that I will never forget as long as I live. I heard her sucking in air as hard as she could. Then utter silence followed. My daughter had stopped breathing.

What runs through a mother's head in a moment like this cannot be described. But I'm sure many of you know what it feels like. The heart stops and we go on autopilot. Somehow, we just know what to do. I yanked Gina out of bed and hopped around the apartment with me trying to wake her up. I remembered reading an article about Sudden Infant Death Syndrome (SIDS) that described what to do that when a child wasn't breathing. Finally, after what seemed like an eternity, Gina opened her eyes. I rushed her to the ER. The diagnosis was asthma. Unbeknownst to me, her father (my ex) had been smoking inside his home during Gina's visits. It aggravated her condition so much that it triggered this nearly fatal attack.

For the next three years, I ran from doctor to doctor and became obsessed with finding a cure to her asthma. I would wake up several times in the night to count her breaths from across the hallway. I believe I am still such a light sleeper because of that. Then one day her asthma went away entirely. I don't know if was because of genetics or because she got stronger as she grew up. But thankfully, my 21-year-old daughter hasn't had an asthma attack since she was seven years old.

THE WOMEN'S CODE TIP

The Main Focus that occupies us right now is probably not going to be around forever. There is a good chance that "This too, shall pass," as a Jewish proverb wisely says. This problem or that issue or the obstacle that we are wrestling with currently is a phase, a rhythm in our lives and is something that inevitably will change or come to an end. This is just now, not forever.

Instead of driving ourselves crazy to finding a way to have it all at once or fix it all at once, the concept of ego-RHYTHM gently brings us back on track to our Main Focus right now.

For example, actress Drew Barrymore said in an article[16] that she "had to give up a lot to be a mother and that some things fall off the table … but what does stay on the table becomes much more important." Her sentiment confirms the concept of ego-RHYTHM. She set a Main Focus, her child is the most important aspect of her life right now. She is in her Mom ego-RHYTHM. Knowing what ego-RHYTHM you are in gives you amazing clarity and focus. It helps you relax and actually enjoy a particular phase of your life. When we give ourselves permission to have a Main Focus (and let what isn't important "fall off the table") then we can finally breathe because life becomes much simpler. All other choices and decisions are made around that.

Knowing our Main Focus gives us the power to assess what phase (or rhythm) of our lives we are currently in. That way we can time our efforts in just the right way that makes it possible to have it all. Not at the same time. At just the right time.

For example, generally I would not recommend that women start a new business after we've just had our first baby. Certainly, we may want to think that we can do both, but two major events that demand our full attention at once will require an incredible amount of energy and support. It could be that we are so exhausted trying to do both that we aren't truly able to enjoy either one. I had no choice but to do both as a single mom, but juggling two major ego-RHYTHMs was not enjoyable.

Below are the 9 Main ego-RHYTHMs that we may cycle through in our lifetime. Some can come around multiple times:

1. Me
2. Career / Education
3. Family and Friends
4. Health
5. Love
6. Mom
7. Bad Luck / Tragedy
8. Transition
9. Zen

I'm sure you've heard the phrase that timing is everything. Well, that is the key to having it all. Timing. You can experience everything you want in this life. There is an optimum time for each phase of your life and ego-RHYTHMs can be proactively chosen or forced upon us.

If you're being introduced to this for the first time, I think it will be helpful to hear from a woman who used the concept of ego-RHYTHM to identify and refocus her life. Here is an example of what it looks like through her eyes.

Christine from Seattle, a married new mother in her mid-thirties and one of the first groups of women who applied the concept of ego-RHYTHM to her life, writes:

> *"'Live in the now' is a phrase I hear constantly. Intellectually*
> *I know that I should—but I never can seem to stop thinking*

about 'what's coming.' ego-RHYTHM gives tools to stop and understand where I am and for how long I'm likely to be here. I appreciate that this doesn't try to change the way I interact with the world (as that does not work for me). It doesn't preach. ego-RHYTHM respects that the way to make a necessary change is to recognize it. Then decide for yourself what you want.

It was also helpful for me to write out what I truly want so that I can focus on them when the time is right. For instance, I see my career is important. But most critical for me right now is being the best mom I can be. That is what will fulfill me most. Thank you for helping me pinpoint that. I was feeling like I've been in knots!"

Christine is not alone. Women often tell me how comforting it is to realize that there are naturally occurring rhythms in their lives. When we work with the natural rhythms rather than swimming upstream or trying to "push the river" we are happier, more relaxed, and it's easier for us to accomplish our goals, dreams, and desires.

When you are in career mode–you focus on that. When you become a new mom, your new ego-RHYTHM gives you permission to dive into the happiness of that aspect of your life. Nothing lasts forever so you may as well be where you are 100%. ego-RHYTHM helps you to enjoy the ride and to be truly present right here and right now. Additionally, we implement ego-RHYTHM to help us to set the right priorities at the right time. It's helps to compartmentalize our busy everyday lives into manageable, doable chunks.

The first step to discover our unique ego-RHYTHM is to find out where in life we are right at this very moment. What is the most important thing that is going on? This is called identifying our starting point. Imagine going into the subway system of a large city that you are visiting for the first time. You know where you want to go. But before you can map out the path, you first must find the red dot, the point on the map that says *You Are Here*. When we know what our starting point is and we know where we want to go, then mapping out the path to get there is easy. Each one of us has a unique starting and end point. We discover our unique path for our individual life: were we are, where we have been, and where we want to go.

To get started I want to share with you my own ego-RHYTHM overview depicted in the graph below.

eGO·RHYTHM	Going On Now	Done It	Importance 1-10	Result
Me ego-Rhythm	●		6	
Career / Education ego-Rhythm	●	● ●	7	
Family & Friends ego-Rhythm				
Health ego-Rhythm	●	●	8	●
Love ego-Rhythm	●		8	
Mom ego-Rhythm		●		
Bad Luck or Tragedy ego-Rhythm		● ● ●		
Transition ego-Rhythm		● ●		
Zen ego-Rhythm				

On the left is the list of ego-RHYTHMs. Next to it is my checkmark or multiple checkmarks where I assigned each a level of importance. As you can see, I was experiencing multiple ego-RHYTHMs at the same time. This meant that I had to look at my day-to-day activities and decide which occupied most of my thinking versus which was the most important rhythm for me. It ended up being my Health ego-RHYTHM. At the time, I was suffering from IBS, an embarrassing digestive disorder, for years. It had become so bad that it occupied a tremendous amount of my time while I searched for a cure, focused on treatments, and generally tried to heal myself with various programs.

Now, it's your turn. In the next chapter you'll be completing your own ego-RHYTHM assessment to discover where you are right now. Then you can start to set your Main Focus and will be in sync with your natural flow. You'll be in control. You won't be wondering what's next or wishing, hoping, or praying that what you are actually doing the right thing at this moment. You'll know.

A Main Focus is in unison with your ego-RHYTHM and compliments it. For example, if you are in your Health ego-RHYTHM your Main Focus is to get well. Any and all decisions that you make, which events you attend, who you want to hang out with, what you eat, how much personal time you need—is based on your Main Focus of getting well. If you are in your Career ego-RHYTHM, your Main Focus is to either get the promotion, open your own business, or advance (whatever that may be for you). Setting a Main Focus assists you to fully appreciate each phase of your life. Read more about how to set a Main Focus in the chapter Getting from Overwhelmed to Awesome.

When you truly understand your ego-RHYTHMs, the pressure is off. No longer will you feel that you have to be everything to everyone. It's impossible to have the body of a supermodel, the career of a CEO, children, a husband, a dog, a perfect home, and the thousands of other things that modern society tells us that we need to have all at once! ego-RHYTHM puts an end to the imposed craziness that causes women to have anxiety attacks and nervous breakdowns. It simply makes life more manageable.

FINDING YOUR OWN EGO-RHYTHM AND WHAT IT MEANS

Modern women are just bombarded. There's nothing but media telling us we're all supposed to be great cooks, have great style, be great in bed, be the best mothers, speak seven languages, and be able to understand derivatives. And we don't really have women we're modeling after, so we're all looking for how to do this.

JAMIE LEE CURTIS, *ACTRESS*

To discover your ego-RHYTHMs, let's first learn more about them.

Me

You're in the Me ego-RHYTHM when it's all about what you want and the redefinition of who you are. Your Me ego-RHYTHM is most likely to occur in your later years, often when women are in their early to mid-forties and the kids are leaving or have left the home. This is when women ask the question, "What about me?"

Career/Education

You are in your Career/Education ego-RHYTHM when your job advancement, work, or education is the most important aspect of your life.

Family and Friends

You are in your Family and Friends ego-RHYTHM when your home life and family, including spending quality time with parents or children, are your primary focus. You might also be focused on being social and being "out and about."

Health

You are in your Health ego-RHYTHM when you have to take care of yourself physically and/or emotionally, or when a close family member needs extended care and you are the caregiver.

Love

You are in your Love ego-RHYTHM when you are looking for or have found the ultimate partner. Getting engaged and married are the focus of this ego-RHYTHM.

Mom

The Mom ego-RHYTHM encompasses having or adopting a new baby, especially the first three years. During this rhythm your sense of self changes until the new definition of you as a mother emerges. You may or may not repeat this rhythm for each of your children.

Bad Luck or Tragedy

The Bad Luck or Tragedy ego-RHYTHM is when nothing seems to go right and a lot of misfortune or plain bad luck happens in succession. It could mean that someone close to you dies or becomes seriously ill, or something happens that is unexpected and unwelcome. Often this period comes just before a major breakthrough and is your ultimate test of how badly you want what you asked for.

Transition

Divorce, a new job, getting fired or laid off, and more all indicate that you are in the Transition ego-RHYTHM. When something ends, but something new hasn't quite started, the in-between phase becomes a life transition. During the Transition ego-RHYTHM, you might focus on trying different things until your life clicks again and becomes clear.

Zen

You're in your Zen ego-RHYTHM when you desire to find God or a spiritual connection with the divine. This rhythm can be a personal journey inward in an effort to find meaning and inner peace, often through being quiet and seeking solitude or through an association with a spiritual or religious group. A sabbatical falls into this category.

Now, you are ready for the ego-RHYTHM Assessment.

Review the ego-RHYTHM assessment graphic and then follow these steps:

- ❀ Checkmark which ego-RHYTHMs that are happening now. Rate them from 1–10 by importance. (Hint: Some ego-RHYTHMs come around several times.)

- ❀ Checkmark which ego-RHYTHMs that you have already been through in the Done It column.

- ❀ Evaluate your list. If it is not immediately obvious what your current ego-RHYTHM is then pay attention to what thoughts or actions preoccupy most of your day. Most likely there is only one main ego-RHYTHM. But if you find there are two of equal importance examine if you are in your Transition ego-RHYTHM.

eGORHYTHM	Going On Now	Done It	Importance 1-10	Result
Me ego-Rhythm				
Career / Education ego-Rhythm				
Family & Friends ego-Rhythm				
Health ego-Rhythm				
Love ego-Rhythm				
Mom ego-Rhythm				
Bad Luck or Tragedy ego-Rhythm				
Transition ego-Rhythm				
Zen ego-Rhythm				

THE WOMEN'S CODE TIP

The answer to having it all is simple. It is ours to have. But we need to learn how to set priorities, and accept universal or divine timing.

Become aware of what rhythm you are in and determine if you have set a Main Focus that matches your ego-RHYTHM. That way you will understand if your actions are supporting your priorities. And if they are not, simply course correct. When we know what our ego-RHYTHM is or when we are entering a new one, all of our decisions are rooted in support of that phase of our life.

No longer will women feel like we have to be two places at once. And even worse, guilty if we aren't. No longer will women have to feel that we aren't enough because we aren't doing enough. Instead, when we follow our ego-RHYTHM we will know that our efforts, focus, and attention is being spent on just the right thing to get us exactly what we want to be at this point in our lives.

We will feel like we are at the right place at the right time. We will know to focus our attention on what we really want. Understanding ego-RHYTHM brings us back to enjoying the present, versus chasing the future.

THE WOMEN'S CODE BONUS GIFT:

To help you even further The Women's Code has created a Bonus Gift for you. If you want more information about ego-RHYTHM just let us know and we'll provide you with our special report "7 Steps to Finding Your ego-RHYTHM." Please visit this page and tell us where to send it. TheWomensCode.com/7-Steps

The night my daughter stopped breathing changed me forever. It was one of my defining moments. When Spirit, God, the Universe or whatever you call it forces us on our knees, we are invited to take a deeper look. Often a strong message like that suggests that we need to take an honest look at our current lives to ask, "What is going on? "What is the lesson?" Or even better, "What is our growth opportunity that is hiding in this event?"

First, I had to fight my own resistance. Let's face it, who wants to search for a lesson or a deeper meaning during challenging and difficult circumstances? Something had taken my daughter's breath away and I needed to pay attention to what that was. I figured it out. I had been angry and disappointed with the circumstances that I had found myself in. Single motherhood was not the life I had wanted. I wanted the cliché, the proverbial dream of the husband, house, and two happy children. Because I didn't get what I wanted, I fought what I had. Once I changed and accepted my life for what it was and I started to become happy with my micro family of two, then my situation improved dramatically. I became a better mother, truly dedicated to my family, and was finally able to enjoy what I had.

During those difficult years, I started to think more about how time and timing affects the way we think and feel about life changing events and our lives in general. For the first time, I realized that a time-based concept really helped me. I realized that there were clear patterns in my life. Not just in obvious things, but more like ebb and flow, the motion of waves, or the seasons. I recognized that we move in a rhythmic pattern. We lease cars for three to four years. Many of us, especially in our defining years, change jobs every couple of years. Our children have defined phases until they move into the next. There are patterns everywhere, especially during our "defining years" that generally are from 25–40 when we decide who we are and what our career and life will look like.

What if these patterns were predictable and happened throughout our lives? And what if we could consciously recognize what these patterns or rhythms mean to us. Would that help us? What if we knew that we were simply entering a new rhythm? We would be able to take a deep breath. What a relief to know that our most challenging ego-RHYTHMs aren't forever. We could relax and focus on our current rhythm, committing fully to it and living more in the present moment.

Imagine a surfer who is out in the ocean waiting for a wave. They never question if there will be another one. Instead, he or she sits and waits patiently until the right wave comes. Isn't that a great attitude to have? To know what is coming and not to worry what it looks like because we have all the skills necessary to ride that next wave, whatever it may be.

I knew that I was onto something. I established the concept and called it ego-RHYTHM because the original Latin meaning of the word ego is self. In that sense the translation of ego-RHYTHM simply refers to one's own self rhythm. It is time to embrace ourselves and The Women's Code fundamental belief is that each of us is perfect the way she is regardless of where she is.

Next, I tested my ego-RHYTHM concept with a group of 50 women ranging from their mid-20s to over 60. I did more testing with other women during my first Women's Code Live Event. The results were always similar, and I saw patterns emerge. As the patterns got clearer it became easier to identify how women have become so overwhelmed, dissatisfied, miserable, and unhappy. So often we tried to manage four or five ego-RHYTHMs at once!

THE CORE CODE
OF CONDUCT

It's okay to be first.

CONDOLEEZZA RICE, *FORMER UNITED STATES SECRETARY OF STATE*

Serious power is new for women. It's only been in the last half century or so that we marched in large numbers through the doors that the Women's Liberation Movement opened. Remember that as recently as the 1960's, women were still fighting in some states to own property and have bank accounts in their names. The Women's Liberation Movement enabled us to achieve success without limits. But nobody taught us what to do with the power that came with it.

It wasn't like women have been groomed since childhood as men have been for generations. No one gave us our rights. We had to demand them and shatter the glass ceiling. We fought and fought hard, blazing our own trail and finding our own way because there were no guides to show us the way. When we did get to the top, we often asked ourselves, "Now what?"

Our foremothers paved many inroads for our success. But they passed the baton onto us to figure out what's next, and frankly, we're not sure where we're going. There's no code of conduct in place that helps women to maneuver—whether it's in the workplace, social circles, home life, or all the other arenas that overlap these days.

Indeed our mentors only had one piece of the puzzle. Their goal was simple—they just wanted to get the same rights for women that men had and that overall movement was called Feminism. So, we listened and got to work, literally and figuratively. We donned our black power suits and stilettos, networked at lunches, joined the daily commute and marched in droves to the workplace to go after gender equality. Feminism promised us that there was greater happiness and fulfillment to be found in the workforce than by staying at home serving our families. We believed the women who told us that when we achieved equality, we would be happy.

THE WOMEN'S CODE TIP

What we forgot was that every generation can only bring us so far. The next generation must make new strides. First we achieved equality. Great! Now, it's up to us to figure out how to balance our careers with our home lives so that we can finally achieve the happiness that our feminist foremothers talked about.

One way to do this is to use all that we have earned—our prestige and influence—to support other women. Because what's happened is that women aren't being good to one another. Instead, we have been treating each other very badly. I hear too many horrific stories about this type of behavior. Perhaps you are nodding in agreement or shaking your head in disbelief or denial. But the truth is that many women aren't using our knowledge to uplift the next talented generation of females. On the contrary, we are crushing them—and often deliberately.

But relief is here. The Women's Code is the missing piece. It's the next phase of feminism which gives us the roadmap and the guidance we need to figure out what our next step is.

It's time for everyone, not only powerful female leaders, to uplift, share and then gracefully pass on our accumulated knowledge and power to the next generation of women. Through The Women's Code we gain the confidence to lead and advance without fear because other women support us. As a former corporate director and a longtime entrepreneur, I see how the lack of a Women's Code produces pettiness, gossip, backbiting, sabotage, and competition in the workplace and beyond.

When I saw how men support each other through an unwritten, underlying code that for the most part they all follow, I thought … where is our code? Where do women come together and agree how to treat each other to support one another? Passed on from one generation to the next, it's almost as if men just instinctively know what to do. They support other men in advancing their careers. They know when to challenge, question, disagree, and keep their mouths shut. They don't even have to talk about it … they just know.

Women, on the other hand, often pretend to listen and support each other but often once we turn our backs it is an entirely different story. Most women would be shocked to hear what is said about them. We tear each other down, we block another woman's career advancements, and we withhold critical information.

Women often think that if it's been tough for us, it should be tough for others. If nobody helped me, why would I help anyone else? I want others to feel the same pain, pay the same dues. Perhaps we were just too busy, too overwhelmed, too frazzled, and too frustrated to see clearly just how much we needed a code. Until now. The Women's Code is here and it is going to change everything.

As I began to develop my own personal thoughts on The Women's Code, I dug deep. I searched through all the pain that I had experienced in my life and the disappointments I had with other women. I wondered how can I turn this around? How can others benefit from this? I began with a shift in my own thinking.

This shift is our new understanding of how women can and should treat other women. The Women's Code has a fundamental Core Code of Conduct. This Core Code is based on the simple idea that we need each other. We ourselves are overdue to accept responsibility for the rise in bullying, gossip, catfighting, brutal competition with each other, and generally being "mean girls."

The Core Code of Conduct includes these principles:

- We are all connected.
- Women need other women for optimum health and success.
- Be aware how your behavior affects others.
- Speak the truth.

- ❀ Don't make up stories.

- ❀ Treat women as you would want your daughter to be treated.

- ❀ Support women in their quest for love, success, and happiness.

- ❀ Mentor women who come after you so that they can take advantage of your trailblazing ways.

- ❀ Let women who have what you want be a source of inspiration.

- ❀ Every woman has her unique talents and flaws.

- ❀ Collaboration builds on each other's strength.

- ❀ Develop confidence and trust your unique talents so you never feel that you have to undermine other women in your quest to achieve more.

- ❀ Every woman who achieves her dream is another woman who can help more women to achieve their dreams.

Without this shift in thinking about how we relate to women, the awareness of why we need to change, and what our own part is in this, we can't move from the position of "every woman for herself" to the concept of uplifting other women around us.

The Three Pillars of the Women's Code help us make these changes to shift our behavior and attitudes. The Three Pillars are: Awareness, Support and Collaboration. When we understand and follow the principles of the Three Pillars it can help us build functioning relationships with women, easily and effortlessly. The Three Pillars are equally applicable in our home and work lives.

The Women's Code and the Three Pillars that support are is a new way to give women the confidence to make our own choices and be satisfied with them.

At the same time, it helps women respect each other's differences and helps us support each other with compassion and without judgment

Simply, it's how we start to build a better world. A happy world.

WHAT IS THE WOMEN'S CODE?

You can spend the rest of your life trying to figure out what other people expect from you, or you can make a decision to let that all go.

MARIA SHRIVER, *JOURNALIST AND AUTHOR*

The Women's Code is a return to our core values. It's about taking responsibility for our lives and choosing to embark on a path where we are free to decide who we want to become and take action to get us there. No longer do women have to simply react to the circumstances around us. Now, women are defining and redefining who we are in this world.

Sometimes before we get to the point where we realize that the future is truly ours, we need to look at and heal the past. My first distrust of women began with my mother. She, like many of our mothers, was the root of my inability to connect with other women. That was a very difficult realization. Just about everything she did sent the message—other women were not to be trusted.

In Europe and in many American families when we get invited it is customary to bring a hostess gift. I remember my Mom telling me, "When a woman brings you yellow roses, it's not friendship. It means she is jealous of you." I watched my mother be so friendly and very talkative to other women to their faces. But behind their backs, she tore them to pieces. When I first noticed her behavior, I remember feeling the distrust. I asked myself, if I can't trust my mother, what woman could I trust? The answer I was taught day in and day out was … none.

Like other people who had a complicated parent-child relationship, I dove in and found great comfort in my work. In my career, I worked unbelievable hours under the false idea that if I became successful, I would finally get the recognition from my mother that I secretly longed for. I was one of the youngest applicants ever to be accepted to the *Bavarian Institute of Fotodesign* in Munich. At 19, I graduated with a degree in photography. Immediately, I secured an internship at the hip German magazine *Wiener*, where I became editor after only two years.

At just 21, I quickly moved on to become photo editor of German *Elle* magazine. This position came with huge responsibilities and everything that goes along with it. Stress, eating disorders, downward glances, judgments, petty office politics—I found myself amongst forty women and a few men competing daily to stand my ground. I was young, inexperienced, and burned out fast. I needed a new start. In 1989, I moved to America to create a new life for myself.

My intention was admirable, but without the foundation of confidence, trust and support, I was lost on how to actually achieve this. I was also envious of women who had what I wanted. I pretended that I was okay, but I wasn't. I simply always found more work and impossible goals to hide behind. I so wanted the proverbial dream of a fulfilling career, loving husband, happy home life, and wonderful female friends to bond with. But when it didn't happen, I buried myself in my work.

Now an adult and a mother myself, as I look back, I can see that my mother was what we call emotionally absent. I also realized that she grew up during World War II. Wartime defined her childhood, and she must have suffered so much because of it. I used to blame her because she was not a "good mother." I decided it was time to take responsibility to create my own future and happiness, even in the face of what I had endured as a child.

The Women's Code teaches us how to get out of our reactive state so we can consciously choose a more proactive one. If I had known then how to create real friendships that genuinely connected me to other women, perhaps things wouldn't have gotten so bad or I wouldn't have felt so lonely.

First, I married a man who wouldn't step up in any way. Neither financially, nor emotionally, and to top it off—he wasn't truthful about his past, either. I certainly recreated the unstable and unpredictable life I knew from before. Pregnant at 27, my journey to the brink began. In 1992, a set of disasters befell me in my new hometown. My decade of bad luck began when I lived in Los Angeles … first there were the riots, then fires, floods, and finally the big Northridge Earthquake.

At 30, I was a single, divorced, unemployed mother. My situation was dire. I had to fight for child support but my ex pushed back hard. I was living month to month in a friend's condo that she had let go into foreclosure. I tried to build a business but I couldn't find clients because Los Angeles was in massive turmoil after all the disasters.

I needed help on every level, but I had no idea how to ask for it, who I could ask or even that I could ask. I didn't any have support because I had no idea how to trust anyone. When I was down on my luck and things didn't go well, I fought against it. I was angry. I was bitter and couldn't believe that I had to deal with one disaster after another. It wasn't fair and it didn't feel right. What did I ever do to deserve such adversity?

My personal dramas weren't just related to my failed businesses. I had major issues with trust that surfaced in my personal life as well. When I was nine months pregnant, I went to see one of the few girlfriends I had at the time. Susanne was a size 14 and always had struggled with her weight. I knew she was constantly dieting and trying to lose weight but I didn't realize how insecure this made her. Over lunch, she took pictures of my plump baby belly when she suddenly sized me up from head to toe and told me how glad she was that I was finally fatter than she was. I was flabbergasted. I calmly replied that I wasn't fat. I was pregnant. To this day I recall this scenario because I still don't know why she said what she did. But it intensified my feelings of distrust towards other women.

Lies. Cutting comments. Betrayals. Why did I continue to meet and befriend women who hurt me so deeply?

One baby step at a time, I managed to get myself together and slowly life started to work again. I rebuilt my photography representation business and found new clients. But I still couldn't connect with other women. Whatever it was about me, I kept experiencing a lot of backstabbing. In fact, I set up my life in a way so that I didn't have to deal with other women. I worked alone, at home and definitely never went on a "girls night out."

But, the incidents kept happening, I was attracting negativity from women.

Back in those days, I represented a photographer who shot for a famous lingerie company. The woman in charge was a very powerful, yet insecure woman. She told the photographer that she just didn't want to talk to me. Ever. But that information never reached me.

One day, I called her to clarify an invoice. After I hung up, I thought the call went well. But ten minutes later, my client furiously asked why I spoke to her and asked what in the world I had said to her. I was dumbfounded. The woman had made up a false story that I called to *renegotiate* his contract. Unfortunately, it put a riff between my client and me. I certainly wasn't surprised when that woman was fired years later because I realized she ruled through tyranny and in the end it cost her job.

So, I escaped deeper into my work. What else was there? With a non-existent personal life as a single parent and business owner, I struggled through years of producing still photography shoots for clients in Los Angeles and representing photographers. Business improved but then some type of setback would happen and I had to start all over again.

All along I kept thinking that there had to be a better way to do this. Was I destined for more of the same problems over and over again? Little did I know that this was just a taste of the grand finale that was yet to come—the ultimate betrayal at the hands of my own employee.

My trusted longtime assistant got too close to a key photographer and he convinced her to take my client list and my outstanding invoices. He paid her to set up her own shop. In just days, I lost the photography representation business that had taken me years to build. The timing couldn't have been worse—during Christmas, no less.

The damage was irrevocable and my reputation was destroyed. I was angry and disappointed. I sued them both. For one year, I fought the battle of my life. I wanted them to pay. Then, six months after the lawsuit was filed September 11th wiped out my production business once again. That was it! It had broken my last ounce of strength. I lost a half a million dollars in gross sales during the lawsuit. And another half a million within 48 hours.

The lawsuit settled a year later and I made out with exactly nothing. After all was said and done and paid, I walked away with zero dollars and had to start all over again. Furiously, I needed to figure out what I wanted to do and how to rebuild my life. Then I got hit with the worst. My father passed away suddenly after a six-week fight with pancreatic cancer. My biggest supporter was gone. I was never more distraught and miserable in my entire life.

So, I returned to my work for solace. I kept my head down and focused on work. And more work. But I was in debt to the tune of $135,000. I don't know how I got through those years, but eventually my hard work paid off when I sold my company to Bill Gates' Corbis Corporation in 2006. It took 13 years of grueling dedication and during that time I worked from dawn to dusk, traveled from coast to coast, and often to Europe, drumming up business while trying to keep my head above water … until I hit the jackpot.

Finally, I was successful and respected. I had it made. Or had I?

I was still coming from a place where I couldn't trust anyone but myself. Yes, I became a multi-millionaire, but it wasn't enough because I was still alone. And being a single mom, not much in my personal life had changed, I still didn't receive many social invitations. In a word, I was still miserable and unhappy.

When you read biographies about people who became hugely successful they all have one thing in common. They *don't* read like this: something good happened, then something even better happened. And voila, finally this great thing occurred that was even better and life was happily ever after. Instead, most successful people's stories read like this. They were down on their luck, things got a lot worse, and on top of that something even worse happened. But with determination and the will to succeed, they came out on the other side.

This is the genesis of The Women's Code. We all need a lifeline to help us succeed when things are tough, and we all need cheerleaders who believe in us. We all need the support of others. This system truly helps women make good choices based on awareness, support and collaboration.

When I began my Women's Code journey, the first thing I decided to do was to give all women a break. A fresh start and a clean slate. Forgiveness all around.

First I forgave all the women I felt who had wronged me. The woman who called me fat when I was pregnant was forgiven. My mother, who made me feel like I was never enough, was forgiven. The woman who sabotaged my career was forgiven.

To be clear, there is a difference between forgiving and forgetting. I no longer dwell on the wrongs but I do remember them as a reminder not go down that road again. Once I let go of every grudge, I felt free and energized. Liberated. I spent more time developing my personal Women's Code. And this is what I did:

I decided that I would no longer be envious of what other women had that I wanted—like a husband, or a traditional family, or lots of relatives visiting during the holidays. Instead, I would make an effort to learn what that woman knows that I don't know that got her to be successful in an area that I am not.

Yes, we realize that every woman has her own set of difficulties in one area or another. And when we can see women not as the enemy, but as people who are just like us we realize that we weren't so different to begin with. And most importantly, I realized that I created my life. Whatever wasn't working for me, I could do my part, take responsibility for it, and create something better for my child and myself.

THE WOMEN'S CODE TIP

Our past experiences shape who we are. When we take responsibility for our life instead of blaming past circumstances we can move forward. Taking charge is a powerful tool.

This action of taking charge frees us from our victim roles. When we learn how to trust other people, especially other women, it will be clear that we alone and not our experiences define our lives.

Along the way, I had significant Aha Moments. When I realized that women are all the same, irrespective of where we come from, I felt a wave of love for other women that I didn't think was possible to feel. I felt overflowing compassion for them. Without these women, even with the adversity they caused, I wouldn't be who I am today.

I discovered that most tyrants hide their insecurities behind power. If these women can relearn how to build their confidence using The Women's Code we just might feel safe enough to lead with integrity, whether we're leading a staff at a hair salon, a restaurant, a massage studio, a classroom or an assembly line.

When women lash out for no apparent reason I compare this to a scared animal that sits trapped in a hole. It's dark. It's scared. It's reacting. It doesn't know if what is coming at it is a poking stick or a helping hand, so the scared animal attacks everything. Rather than reacting to what comes at us, with The Women's Code we can step out in front of it without fear.

Thus, the Women's Code journey begins. It helps us by raising our awareness, dissolving rivalry, jealousy, dishonesty, toxic behavior, fear, denial and the hoarding of information and power. It opens the door to find your true self, so you can start living your life, making more money, and finding everyday balance and clarity on your path.

The Women's Code helps women start to trust each other again. It teaches us to accept and understand other women's choices, which establishes mutual respect. That does not mean we must agree with other people's choices. Rather we come to an understanding about where someone else is coming from. Simply, it lets us communicate and collaborate on a neutral level.

So how does it work?

Firstly, it's important to note that The Women's Code doesn't tell women what we should do. Instead, it empowers us to identify for ourselves what the most important aspect of our life is right now. That way, you can exude confidence and happiness because you love who you are, your life, and everyone in it.

Next, the ego-RHYTHMs that you learned about enable you to see more clearly where you are in your life, so you can focus on what's important to you instead of worrying about what you may still want or what appears to be missing. Modern women are extraordinarily complex. We can do five things at once, and look like we're in control. Because we seem to be in control, we think that we can take on more than we were ever supposed to do, which doesn't add to our happiness, as we've pointed out in previous chapters.

The Women's Code is a new leadership model, a foolproof fix for work, love, family and play that creates camaraderie and a new sisterhood amongst women. It's a new baseline, an agreed upon set of principles that uses our power to uplift all women. It reinstalls trust within our gender and reconnects women.

How The Women's Code Works

- ❋ Find your ego-RHYTHM, which determines where you are right now.
- ❋ Sync your Main Focus to your ego-RHYTHM
- ❋ Act according to the Core Code of Conduct
- ❋ Decide what you want, which determines where you want to go.

- ❀ Establish a good Work-Life Balance by utilizing the (Life) Balance Plan
- ❀ Map it out to determine your personalized blueprint to assess how to get from where you are to where you want to be

The Women's Code dusts off feminism and modernizes it. It's time to redefine who we are, what we are, and what we want. The Women's Code helps women lead through heightened awareness, support and collaboration which creates relief in our lives. At our core, we all want to be loved, accepted, and to live a life with connection, purpose, and passion.

> The Women's Code is here to support you.
> You don't have to do more.
> There isn't a single idea that you must follow.
> There are no "musts."
> There is no guru.

On the contrary, women create their own code. You, me, and every other woman on this planet can develop their own personal code that will in turn, help support other women. When we can bond, trust, and be successful together our life is no longer a battlefield.

Instead, when we follow the Three Pillars, the principles and the Core Code of Conduct for The Women's Code we turn our lives into a series of positives, not only for ourselves, but also for everyone around us.

Life also becomes fun, relaxed and more carefree.

DEFINING WHAT YOU WANT, TO GET WHAT YOU WANT

When you create, you might as well think big.
It takes the same effort.

BEATE CHELETTE, *ENTREPRENEUR AND AUTHOR*

So many women tell me that when they started applying the principles of The Women's Code life became more fun. They felt safe to re-connect to women again. Their defenses came down and they had more energy. They got healthier and felt better about themselves. Their newfound confidence and ability to trust affected all their other relationships as well.

For example, our own studies show that women who completed either The Women's Code Live or Online programs see a 65% improvement in their relationships with other women and their significant others. The Code helps you shape your own social and family lives in a way that enlivens you.

We've covered the importance of defining what success and happiness mean for you. Have you begun to define it? To be successful and experience balance in our lives, first we must consciously discover what that means to us. What is a good balance for you?

How can we recognize what constitutes being in balance or being successful if we don't know what it looks like, or worse, if it remains a moving target somewhere in our future?

A fundamental principle of The Women's Code is defining what we want and then devising a plan of action to make it happen. First, we get clear about what we want. Again, if we can't identify it we can't fulfill it. And if we can't fulfill it, we will forever be searching for it, which puts happiness far away in the future. It always feels just out of reach. But The Women's Code puts our happiness back within our grasp.

The concept is easy. When a friend gave me the most astonishing bouquet of flowers she said that she was very disappointed with my reaction. She said that I didn't know how to experience joy over something simple like receiving flowers. This was a huge wake-up call for me. I realized that I had forgotten how to enjoy the little things that can make life so pleasant. Even though my friends and other people did nice things for me, something inside of me wasn't able to connect to joy.

Once I realized that I added to my own misery by not knowing how to have a good time, I changed my attitude. I made a list of what I wanted to make me happy. And when I got even one tiny little bit of it, I made a big deal about recognizing it and enjoying the moment.

On my vision board (which I'll explain in just one moment) I put a picture of a huge turtle swimming in the ocean. Two years ago my daughter and I went to Hawaii and a gigantic turtle swam right beneath us. What a powerful, joyful moment to realize that what I had wanted was just given to me. That is what brings happiness, it's our recognition that we get little by little what we have wished and asked for.

ego-RHYTHM shows you where your red dot *You Are Here* starting point is. The Want-It-All List will help you to identify what you uniquely want to create for yourself. Be aware that sometimes we think we want something and upon further examination we find out that it wasn't really what suits us.

Here is an example.

Phoebe from Pasadena, CA participated in one of The Women's Code Online Courses. She shared that she joined the course because she felt that she needed to pay more attention to her business, a small Skin Spa with personalized skin care for private clients. During our live coaching sessions, Phoebe, who is in her late fifties, admitted that she recently found a new love interest. She felt guilty for not putting in the required time for her business to get it to where it could be.

Her new man wanted to spoil her in every possible way including trips and quality time together. She was having more fun than she ever had before and was giddy with excitement about the joy this new relationship brought into her life. Ultimately, Phoebe realized that what she really wanted was to enjoy the relationship and make that her priority. Phoebe gave herself permission to be fully in the moment and experience her new relationship to the fullest. She used The Women's Code to find out that what she really wanted and found out it was something different than what she originally thought. With the support of her sisters, the other women in the course, she realized that there was nothing wrong with wanting one thing more than another. Last I heard she is still traveling and enjoying herself tremendously.

When women look at our lives in broad strokes it causes stress. We generalize our desires in broad terms like a great relationship, a fulfilling job, and more time for ourselves. But we fail at truly defining what that looks like and feels like. So, how can we know when our goals are so broad they are hardly identifiable? And it's hard to ask for help when we feel the task is too monumental to put on someone else.

Instead, we can get clarity and claim what it is that we want. We can then execute a step-by-step plan to achieve it.

THE WOMEN'S CODE TIP

Like attracts like. The more we become who we want to be, we will attract others who support and elevate our gender as well.

To help you get clarity, The Women's Code uses our simple Want-It-All List. It is a beautifully designed, ready to use, printable worksheet to create your list. We even added our Top Tips so that you can avoid some common mistakes when creating your list.

THE WOMEN'S CODE BONUS GIFT:

Please go to this page:
TheWomensCode.com/Want-It-All,
and download your Want-It-All List. Or find out
how to get your Want-It-All postcard for free.

Some women like to use a Vision Board, which is where you cut out images or words and create a digital or physical collage of what you want. Personally I use a Vision Board that I change every year according to my desires and it is visible to me daily, posted right in my workspace. Other women like to use software called Mindmovies[17] where you can create a video of your dream life.

The Women's Code gives you the Want-It-All List that includes suggestions that you can use, change, and make your own. It's fun to think about what we want. What sounds good to you? More romance by going out with our partner more frequently? Better self-care through going to the gym three times a week? The new 328 BMW to tool around in? Let loose and start to visualize what your ideal life looks like.

My **Want-It-All** List:

_____	**Grow My Business**
_____	_____
_____	_____
_____	_____
_____	**ABUNDANCE**
_____	_____
Buy a House	_____
_____	_____
_____	_____
_____	_____

Improve Relationship
One at Sea
Prosperity
Get In Shape
Get Married
Meet a new People
Family
Health
Go Dancing
INTIMACY
SAVE MONEY
Find a Hobby
Volunteer
Start Writing
Faith
Kids
Spend More Time With My Kids
Friends
More $$$

TheWomensCode.com
office@BeateChelette.com
US + 310 558 4248

72

GETTING FROM OVERWHELMED TO AWESOME

I think that somehow, we learn who we really
are and then live with that decision.

ELEANOR ROOSEVELT, *FORMER FIRST LADY OF THE UNITED STATES*

This is where we tie all the different aspects of The Women's Code together to help you get where you want to go in life. Certainly, our lives can feel overwhelming because there is so much all vying for our attention at once. Between kids, relationships, and careers, we juggle an enormous amount of responsibility on a daily basis. Often, our own superhuman expectations of what we should be capable of pushes us to the edge of our sanity. We try to do it all at once, but nobody can be a perfect housewife, mother, and career woman, not at the same time. We added a second work shift to days that were already brimming with activities from childrearing, community service, caregiving, and homemaking.

But this stress is because women were trying to do it all, all at once. And now you know differently. You know that there is a natural rhythm to your life called ego-RHYTHM. Any overload gets much easier when we implement the ego-RHYTHM concept into our lives. Realizing where you are and what ego-RHYTHM you are in makes life more manageable. Suddenly, more can fall "off the table" to create time for what is really important.

All the different components of The Women's Code are designed to work together seamlessly. Knowing your ego-RHYTHM is the basis for discovering where you are in your life journey right now. The 9 ego-RHYTHMs establish the Main Focus of your life in your particular rhythm. If you are in a Mom ego-RHYTHM, your children are the most important focus in your life. If you have a health issue like cancer or a digestive disorder like I did in my Health ego-RHYTHM, then that is where your Main Focus should be. Your Main Focus will change based on which ego-RHYTHM you are experiencing.

When you know what your Main Focus is, you determine your priorities based on one and only one criteria. Do your decisions bring your closer to or further away from your Main Focus? That is what you want to ask yourself now. For example, if you are in your Health ego-RHYTHM and your boss asks you to work overtime, ask yourself—does this help or hurt me? Based on your answer, you decide whether you will do it. Or not. And if you have any issues saying that magical word—*no*, help is here. In the chapter on Support, I'll go over specific language techniques you can use to say no to what isn't supporting your Main Focus.

When we are clear on what is the most important aspect of our lives right now it's easier to make choices that truly are in our best interests. Women, myself included, generally try to do too much. Understanding our ego-RHYTHM is how we stop the inner argument that pushes us to do more—even when we are doing all that is humanly possible and there just isn't room on our plate for anything more.

One of the graduates of a Women's Code Online Course told me that she had gone through years of therapy to deal with her inability to say no to her mother's constant demands. Finally, with this simple idea, she asked herself if acquiescing to her mother's request was good for her. Or not. Suddenly she knew how to say, no thanks. This is not what I need, nor want to do. It amazes me how many of us have never asked ourselves the question, should I agree to this? Or is this the right thing for me? Or does it make me feel good? Should we really drive two hours to our sister's house cook and clean and help prepare for the family reunion when we are not feeling well? If the answer is no, now can you can say it. That is how The Women's Code helps us to create a healthy Work-Life Balance. We act instead of reacting.

THE WOMEN'S CODE TIP

We learn how to say no to what doesn't support our Main Focus, and this gives us so much more time in the day to say yes to what actually supports our Main Focus. We learn to balance our lives because we start taking better care of ourselves.

The concept of this continuous movement of ego-RHYTHMs gives us peace of mind. We know whatever it is that is going on right now, especially if we are in one of the difficult rhythms, won't last forever. The rhythm eventually ends and we move into another ego-RHYTHM. Perhaps next we're on the fast track in our career or an unexpected romantic relationship sweeps us off our feet.

The most important thing to know is where you are in your life and to understand that other women will have different ego-RHYTHMs. You could be in your Career ego-RHYTHM, whereas your co-worker just had her baby and is in her Mom ego-RHYTHM. Each of you has a different Main Focus. With this awareness you can collaborate with her more compassionately because this rhythm won't be her priority forever. And career will not be your priority forever, either.

This deep understanding and fundamental awareness that each of us are in different ego-RHYTHMs and have set a different Main Focus is a huge game changer. We can support each other and respect other women's choices to be loyal to their own unique rhythms. No longer do we roll our eyes when our co-worker has to leave at 4:45 p.m. to make it to daycare by 5 p.m., when we wanted to finalize a project by the end of the day. We have a right to our own Main Focus, and so do other women.

Understanding another woman's right to her own ego-RHYTHM and her own Main Focus takes the friction out of our interactions with others. We don't need to show off, force someone into submission, trump them, or make them feel stupid or inadequate any longer because we respect her circumstances hope she will respect ours. This is a much more powerful solution to manage interpersonal relationships.

We know we can and should want different things at different times in our lives. We have become aware of our own choices or simply a naturally occurring rhythm in our lives. We are aware of other women's choices as well. We support what they do because they support what we do.

The core elements of the Women's Code are rooted in the Core Code of Conduct, which we can trust and fall back on. In its simplest form don't do unto others what you don't want done to yourself. If you don't want your colleagues to talk behind your back, you probably shouldn't be talking about them behind their back, either. If you want to be treated with respect in the bank or post office, you should treat the bank teller and post office worker with respect, too. This is the basic energetic principle of what goes around comes around. And as you change, the world around you changes. When you smile, the world smiles with you.

You may need a few tries to get this principle to kick in. Be gentle with yourself. It's okay to not be perfect right away. A series of many small steps will lead you to the goals you identified in your Want-It-All List. If you haven't done that yet, now is a good time to go back and fill it out. It will help you focus and get clear on what is most important to you.

Women no longer need to be so judgmental of each other's choices. Instead we can mutually support each other and accept where women are more easily. If our friend just had a baby, she should be enjoying motherhood to the fullest. When we support her in that choice she supports us in return. Suddenly, we are collaborating with compassion in all of our circles. It could be the tennis club, a knitting circle, an entrepreneur's lunch group, or in our families.

In the next three chapters I am going to introduce The Three Pillars of The Women's Code. They aid in our fundamental understanding of how we rebuild, connect, and interact with each other. For any situation where we contemplate a course of action the formula is the same: awareness of what is going on, assessment of support, and a plan to collaborate so we don't have to do or solve it all ourselves anymore. By following the Three Pillars we learn how to allow others to have their own opinions while we can communicate ours more efficiently.

The circumstances of our lives are what they are because of the choices we have made. Even today, I wouldn't trade in most of my worst moments and biggest painful mistakes because they shaped who I am and how I see my life.

Imagine a day where everyone in our professional and private lives accepts and supports our choices. And in return, we accept other women's life choices, knowing that all of society benefits from them. What a relief, knowing that we all have a place at the table. It's time to learn how to respect and trust each other's different ways of life. Life isn't static. It is in a constant rhythmic motion. Denying that right to ourselves means that we are boxed in and may stay stuck in the past, defending old viewpoints that do not serve us anymore or trying in vain to prove that we are or were once right about an issue. Why wouldn't we want to give ourselves the right to change our opinion or viewpoint as our lives change? Now when you hear someone say, "She sure has changed since she got married," you understand that this woman is living her Relationship/Love ego-RHYTHM. Indeed, she should be acting differently because her Main Focus changed. You can chime into that conversation by saying, "Yes, she's enjoying this new rhythm of her life."

Change is okay. It's natural. It's a constant in our lives. The Three Pillars of The Women's Code help us negotiate the changes in our lives when our Main Focus shifts alongside our ego-RHYTHM. With Awareness we identify where we need a helping hand. Next we learn how to ask and enlist proper Support. Then we can Collaborate for maximum results. This is the magical one-two-three punch that can take us from frustrated and overwhelmed to in control, balanced, and feeling awesome.

AWARENESS: THE FIRST PILLAR OF THE WOMEN'S CODE

Circumstances don't define you.
You define your circumstances.

BEATE CHELETTE, *ENTREPRENEUR AND AUTHOR*

Awareness is The First Pillar of The Women's Code for a good reason. It means being conscious, cognizant, and awake to ourselves and our place in the world. It's this awareness that helps us take control of our circumstances to create new ones. Awareness is the first step to get in front of our lives and move forward in the direction we always wanted to go.

Awareness can begin with a childlike curiosity. We can begin by asking lots of questions. Probe. Examine. Test. Try. Is this relationship really working for me? Am I happy in my current job? Do others see and hear me? Do I feel supported? Is there something more I should see or pay attention to than what is in front of me?

Awareness means holding a mirror to our lives and seeing it honestly. The Women's Code takes a gentle look at where you are versus where you wish you were. Imagine this visual: we may want to start small with a pocket-sized mirror when we do our first evaluation. We start with a few questions and give honest answers about our job, body image, or our relationships. Or if we are ready to take on more than one area of our life we can bring out the wall to ceiling mirror and see everything for what it really is. Only you truly know what you are ready to see. So take your time. Each step forward gives you the courage to take another.

Awareness is the first step to gain more clarity about what is going on. Here's an example. A former team member of my company Beateworks, which sold to Bill Gates' Corbis Corporation, confided in me that she had lost over sixty pounds. Lynda showed me a picture of herself and she pointed out how seriously overweight she had been before. For years Lynda said that she was in denial. It was only when she admitted to herself how out of control her weight truly was that she had the power to change and the weight came off. She wasn't successful in her weight loss attempts before because she wasn't yet aware of where her red dot was that pointed out so clearly *You Are Here.*

A hard, honest look at our self can be sobering and often uncomfortable. I remember the painful realizations when I stayed too long in a relationship or was overly engaged in a business venture that fell through. At first, I beat myself up. I wondered out loud how could I have been so stupid? Shouldn't I have known better? Well, no. I couldn't have done better, I wasn't ready yet. Only when I was ready to hold up the mirror and see how unhappy I was with my partner I could do something about it and walk away from the relationship.

We do the best we can with the information that is available to us at the time. As we become more aware, new information comes to light and we can do things differently—when we are ready.

THE WOMEN'S CODE TIP

Awareness is a light in the dark. It doesn't have to be painful. It can be a gentle nudging that shows us what the next step is in our lives.

Let's have the courage to dig deep. Let's look, see, ask questions. Let's turn on the light that allows us to see our lives as they truly are so we can course correct without wasting another moment in situations that don't serve us.

In our awareness, we realize that we have two choices. We can continue to blame others and point fingers at people or incidents from our past. But that keeps us stuck in the past as a victim. Instead, we can boldly step in front of any situation and see what our part is and assess what we can do to create a better outcome in the future.

Awareness is not about judging what you see as good or bad, success or failure. When we look in the mirror, we make a loving and honest assessment because this is just us, no justifications, finger pointing or blaming others is needed. It is our own heart-to-heart. This is an important step to shine a light on the areas in our lives where there is discomfort. It's not meant to overwhelm you and you don't have to jump into any action right away. Simply start by acknowledging your new viewpoint.

Here is an example how I personally used awareness to improve my ability to lead. I realized that a good testament to my ability to lead would be by seeing what work my team returned to me. If my expectations weren't fulfilled correctly, the old me would have—and did—judge my team. I would have blamed them, saying that they just didn't get it. Or I might have thought that they weren't up to the task. I might have been tough on them and called them out on it in front of others during a meeting. But this would have meant that I assumed that I had done everything right. And the others were to blame. Not me. I was the boss after all, I could call it how I wanted to, right?

Awareness taught me that I was not always right. Now, I have a different approach. I realize that each of my team members is very capable and very smart. Otherwise why would I have hired them? If they are not performing the task to my liking or incorrectly—perhaps I am to blame. If I gave excellent instructions and was very clear about what I asked them to do, wouldn't a smart person be able to deliver it?

Of course they would.

The fault might be mine. Awareness taught me that I have what I lovingly call a "helicopter brain" that can take off in a completely different direction when given the opportunity. My team members were too polite to tell me when I was doing it and after a meeting, often they were left trying to piece together incomplete information.

The way the Three Pillars of The Women's Code resolve an issue like that is easier than you might think. With awareness, I am clear that I am not always specific enough with my instructions. Do I like the fact that I do that? Of course not! But now I know and I can support my team by admitting that this is who I am. It also gives my team permission to help me help them. They can interrupt me, bring me back on topic, and feel free to ask clarifying questions. In return, they get better support from me because they know what they need to do and know how to get the information they need to do their job. That leads us to better collaboration.

This honesty that the first Pillar creates through Awareness allows us to create, lead, and participate in a team, a circle of friends, or even have a family who will go walk over fire for us. Why? Because honesty builds mutual respect and understanding continues to grow. Other people will believe in you and what you stand for.

If you are not getting what you want in your personal or professional life, could it be that what you do is misinterpreted because you are not clear?

My mother, who grew up during World War II, learned that it was not polite to want or ask for *anything*. To get around that she would talk about herself in the third person alluding to "someone" needing "something". But it was about her. She often left us baffled because we had no clue what she was talking about. Looking back, I can only imagine how disappointed she must have been when "someone" couldn't give her what she really needed. Today I nudge her to be more specific and ask her point blank what she means and what she wants. It can be very difficult to state clearly what we need, especially if we don't know what that is.

While beginning your Awareness process here are a few questions you can ask yourself:

> *What's working?*
> *What's not?*
> *What stays?*

What goes?
Who supports me?
What supports me?
Who and what is a drain?

When the results come back, simply acknowledge them and let it be. Take a deep breath. Or ten. You may find that there is some work to be done. But again, go easy with this. This isn't a race. Awareness is a continual process.

Knowing your ego-RHYTHM adds to your awareness. Whether you decide to be a career woman, stay-at-home mom or something else; each choice has tremendous value. It is part of our newfound awareness. Every woman has her unique ego-RHYTHM, her own Main Focus, so it's never a question of being right or wrong. Awareness teaches us to honor where each of us is in the different stages of our lives. That removes the friction in our daily interactions. It offers another way of looking at life rather than judging others.

To become even more self-aware The Women's Code offers these 5-Steps.

Step One: *Awareness. See it for what it is. Ask: Where am I right now?*
Step Two: *Don't judge. Ask: What are my priorities?*
Step Three: *Take responsibility. Ask: Where do I start?*
Step Four: *Design the life you want. Ask: Where do I want to be?*
Step Five: *Devise a plan for change. Ask: What do I need to do to get there?*

Awareness restores our vision. We see what is. We see where we are. The red dot that says *You Are Here* gives us our starting point

We do the best we can moment by moment. We make a choice. Then we make another choice based on where we are in the moment. We are not afraid to change our mind. We evolve and we grow. We are free. We flow with our natural rhythms.

THE WOMEN'S CODE BONUS GIFT:

To help you increase your level of awareness, I have created The Women's Code 7 Keys for each of the Three Pillars. You can go to this page TheWomensCode.com/7-Keys and download the 7 Keys to Awareness for added support in taking this important first step.

My favorite example of how The Women's Code creates seeds of awareness on many different levels comes from 15-year old Melody who, during a Women's Code Live Event, shared her story with the audience. I invited Melody because I wanted to show the audience a little about awareness in action.

A 15-year-old teenager in combat boots stood before the audience and spoke with hardly any emotion about how her mother was fighting for her life in the last stages of cancer. Melody talked about how she knew that her mother was going to die and that she was too young to get a job to make money to pay for experimental treatments. In her mind, that was the only thing she could have done. But there are no jobs for 15 year olds and there was nothing she could do about anything. Melody has no hope for a better life, no role model to aspire to be, and her self-esteem had been destroyed by tragic circumstances.

Every single woman in attendance was touched for her own reasons. Instant awareness was created on multiple levels. Awareness that the youngest among us was hurting the most. Awareness about how early some of us had to face a Tragedy ego-RHYTHM like the one Melody was experiencing. Awareness that some of the women had gone through similar challenges. They could relate to her and they did. So many audience members helped Melody with advice because they overcame obstacles like hers and had support to offer. It may sound corny but it was a magic moment, one that nobody who was there that day has ever forgotten.

In our newfound increased awareness there is usually a pleasant surprise. I had invited Melody, perhaps selfishly, to help me drive a very important point home, which is to be aware that each of us has a story, and that we never know what that story might be. To my great surprise, the next morning Melody was the very first person back at the event. I asked her why she had come back and Melody replied, "Before yesterday, I didn't think that there was a different way to think about my life. Now, I know there is another way."

What Melody showed me and every other woman in the room that day is that The Women's Code works. When the seeds of awareness are planted, even when it happens accidentally, they effortlessly grow into something beautiful and can be so meaningful for us.

SUPPORT: THE SECOND PILLAR OF THE WOMEN'S CODE

I like women. I support women.
I'm like a human bra.

TINA FEY, *COMEDIAN AND WRITER*

Today's women are often exhausted and overwhelmed. We may feel trapped in our lives, wondering if there is something else, something better *out there.* We don't get enough support and at times it appears as if we haven't had any in a long time even if the possibilities are right there for us.

Our first step is to identify what we need and ask for support. We will also look at the different ways men support women, and how the lack of support from other women has hurt us. Then you'll learn how you can rebuild your support system so you never feel alone again.

Support can be offered to us in so many different ways. I have often noticed that we don't always know how to accept support or even recognize it when it arrives. Here is a simple example. My daughter was baking her famous chocolate chip cookies and her boyfriend eagerly asked her if he could help. Instead of accepting his support and assigning him a simple task Gina told him that she was completely capable of baking cookies by herself.

Some of us were taught that if someone helps us then we are weak or that they own us. Do we think there is a big accounting system in the sky where every ounce of help we receive must be repaid in full and with interest? Many women are actually afraid of receiving support for this very reason.

I wish every woman on the planet was able to ask for and receive support, but it's not that simple. Many women are so used to going it alone and taking on more than is humanly possible that we don't know any other way. I remember how my past choices and bad luck pushed me to the bottom. For years, without support or even the awareness that I needed support, I limped along through life.

I was skittish, cautious, and almost expected to be stabbed in the back. That was how my life was before I knew how to identify, ask for, and receive the support that I needed. For so many years, I was totally incapable of asking for help. It never even crossed my mind that I could. And when it came my way, I wasn't entirely sure if I could trust it.

When we are injured or hurt, we can easily fall into fight or flight defense mechanisms. We may even pretend that the way things are going is actually okay. On the inside, we are suffering and we get stuck in a downward "it's only me" spiral. Certainly, our life is the result of our choices, but we didn't think that it was going to ever be this darn hard.

We can develop a system of better support for ourselves. To help you identify the support you need, again go back to your ego-RHYTHM. What is it right now? Where should your Main Focus be? Start there. It's too overwhelming to operate from the feeling that you need to have everything right now.

Which area do you need more help and support with? With your household and with grocery shopping, cooking, or cleaning? Supervising your children's homework, getting to practice, or getting them to and from school? Do you need more time for yourself to work out, go shopping, to get your hair done, or to simply do nothing?

Is it emotional, financial, logistical, or professional? The more we narrow it down the more it becomes possible, and we shake off that overwhelmed feeling like no one can help us because it's all too much. Break it down. Let's examine each area of life step-by-step.

Next, we identify who can support us. If we have a financial question, it's best not to run it by a friend who is in debt. We want to match our support requests to people who have it to give. Who can help us in each of the categories that we just identified? Can our children help out around the house more? Can our husband, brother, sister, mother, or father get involved with supervising homework or driving tasks? Can we change gyms to find one with babysitting, or find a local teenager to take the kids to the park for two hours while we go to the hairdresser?

Then we ask for support. There is an art to asking for support so that we are heard and understood by others. We don't want to make it appear as if we are stating demands. When we have identified what another person can contribute to balance our load it is so much easier to tell them. When we say, can you please take care of dinner twice a week, it is much more effective than telling your husband that he never does anything. This Saturday from 2 to 4 p.m., I am getting my hair done can you please watch the kids beats saying I never have any time for myself, I can't even get my hair done. The more specific you are the easier it will be to get support because you break it down in bite sizes. Let's also recognize that many people around us *want* to help us, and want to support us if only we could tell them how!

My close friend Dr. Marilyn Joyce, The Vitality Doctor™, teaches heart-centered support. This method comes into play when you want to offer to help someone else and it goes like this:

Avoid telling the other person what they should or ought to do. Don't offer suggestions. For example, your girlfriend just told you that she is stressed out over an issue at work. You may suggest that your girlfriend go for a workout with you, because that is what helps you to manage stress, but all she needs is to catch up on some sleep. When offering suggestions that start with "What you should do," or "You ought to do this," we try to fix it for them in our way. That rarely works and it frustrates and drains both sides.

Instead, ask supporting questions like, "What do you need from me?" and "How can I help you with this?" Because when you are asking it opens the flow and effectively increases energy.

Did you know that the more specific you are in your request the more support you will receive? Carol found out at a Women's Code Live Event. During a self-awareness exercise she broke out into tears and confided to the room that she felt guilty about taking a simple bubble bath because there was always so much to do. I led her through some questions and she figured out how she could ask to be supported by her family for some much needed alone time.

The next morning Carol arrived looking more rested and relaxed. She proudly announced that she had asked her family to give her thirty minutes of quiet time in the only bathroom in their apartment. She had enjoyed every minute of her luxurious bath before she came to the event. I wasn't surprised to hear that her family was more than happy to respond to her specific request for thirty minutes of quiet time. This small step—asking for time for a simple thirty minute bath—gave Carol the confidence that she could ask for support in other more critical areas of her life as well. It was a step in the right direction and one worth celebrating. She found relief by turning a general plea for help into one tangible request for support.

Women can still be trailblazers and ask for support. As I was developing The Women's Code, I encountered more than my fair share of roadblocks, writer's blocks, self-doubt, and of course people who told me that I couldn't do it. For a while I reverted back to my old ways and thought I'd have to do it alone. But I found that when I asked for support in clearer terms, I got what I asked for. I was actually enjoying myself along the way. And much of that support, I'm proud to say, came from men.

While in some of my darkest moments in the creation of this book, it was a man who pulled me out of my lady cave (yes, women can also go into caves) and put me back on track. What I learned is that support from men is much different from women, but just as necessary. One of my supportive male friends, Jack Thompson, who loved The Women's Code from the very beginning pointed out during one of my particularly intense breakdowns all the things I did wrong and gave his advice on how to fix it. He even had done research and come up with "the plan" to fix everything. Although what I really needed was a shoulder to lean on, it was an eye-opener. He obviously cared, but seriously?

My friend Alice reminded me that men inherently like to "save" women. The knight in shining armor is slumbering in each of them, ready to step in when a damsel is in distress. That's how men show us they care, always ready to rescue us. Jack, like all the other men who gave me advice, was *not* trying to tear me down by telling me where I had failed. He was coming to my *rescue!* He was just operating within the "man code" on how to show support. Men offer support in a different way than women and here is how.

Generally, men will only give you advice if asked. Unsolicited advice is strictly prohibited because under The Men's Code that means that you would challenge a man's competence. That is why men won't offer unsolicited advice to each other. When a man asks another man for his opinion he is giving him permission to tell him what to do and then he should heed that advice or he may not get it again.

When women approach a man and say things like "I don't know what to do," or "What do you think?" under The Men's Code we just did the equivalent of asking them to tell us how to fix it. Because they are our knights they hear that we are in distress and must be saved. Therefore, it is easy for them to go overboard with their 'fixing' advice. They point out *everything* that needs fixing often in great painful detail. Next time it happens try to remember it comes from a good place and try to understand that.

The problem is, more often than not, this is the exact opposite of what a woman wants when she asks a man for support. **We want to be heard, not fixed.** So it's important to realize what kind of support you need. Do you want emotional support or are you are ready to get in there, troubleshoot, and make a plan? In your request for support, you might want to put in what type you are looking for. For example you can ask a man, "Can I vent to you about a few things? I'm not ready to fix anything but I'd feel better just to let it out." Or if you're ready to hear a different plan, tell him. Get ready. I've found that men will put their heart and soul into helping women when they ask. But again, the trick is to give clear instructions as to what you want a man to do. This is one of the reasons why men love The Women's Code and support it 100% because it makes it easy for them to help.

Men support other men and have been doing so for generations. It is genetically embedded in their DNA. Albeit painfully funny, I think this joke is the perfect example of just how much men support men and how women could learn a thing or two from them.

"A woman didn't come home one night. The next morning she told her husband that she had slept over at a friend's house. The man called his wife's 10 best friends. Not one of them knew anything about it.

A man didn't come home one night. The next morning he told his wife that he had slept over at a friend's house. The woman called her husband's 10 best friends. Eight confirmed that he had slept over and two said he was still there."

Right or wrong, men stick up for each other and they stick together. That's part of their code. The same can't always be said for women.

Why is that?

During my research on interpersonal relationships an interesting fact emerged. Men are very strategic about who they befriend outside their inner circle. Even if they don't particularly like a guy, a man may still choose to spend time with that person for personal or professional advancement. That person may be powerful or be a gateway to meet important people. He can help with networking, or already be a member of and the missing link to get into a valuable private club, team or association.

This idea of building strategic relationships is rooted in their history. When men went hunting or had to defend their tribes, they had to work together. The selection was not based on likes or dislikes or favors, but rather on skill. Jack was the best shot. Jim was the fastest runner. Bill was the strongest. George was the strategist who pulled it all together. Each of them had a particular function to fulfill. It didn't matter if they liked each other. Survival was at stake and men had a common goal. They supported each other because they didn't come together for personal "feel good" reasons. They needed each other, and each appreciated and respected the other for their skill. They knew that the sum of their combined individual skills made them better. They were stronger together.

But the story of women supporting each other is very contrary. Throughout history, women had a different objective. We had to take care of, manage and defend to the best of our abilities our possessions, our children, and our home. We also needed to protect what we had against other women who were looking for or had to replace a provider. This was vital for our survival.

While women naturally had to work together to some degree, we primarily needed each other for moral and emotional support. We may have gone to the river to fetch water together but each of us carried her own water buckets. Each of us took care of her own household and raised her own children. We wanted a community to share but did not need strategic relationships to accomplish big life or death tasks.

This need for community is in a woman's DNA. You may have heard the statistics that men live longer when married but women live longer when we have girlfriends and community. In a study of Behavioral Responses to Stress in Females, Dr. Laura Cousino Klein[18], says: "Study after study has found that social ties reduce our risk of disease by lowering blood pressure, heart rate, and cholesterol. There's no doubt that friends are helping us live longer." [19]

That's why not being able to trust or be supported by other women is also physically hurting women as well. When women get together we produce oxytocin, which is a bonding hormone. In fact, when we aren't bonding, it increases our stress levels. That would explain the statistics about declining female happiness that I cited earlier. If we are alone and cannot connect with other women, we are suffering.

Science supports this. UCLA published a report on the importance of female friendships. Gail Berkowitz writes[20], "Scientists now suspect that hanging out with our friends can actually counteract the kind of stomach-quivering stress most of us experience on a daily basis."

What does that mean for us?

It confirms what we already know. Women need other women. A conversation with a girlfriend can help us work through a difficult relationship issue or a problem at work. It reduces our stress levels and sometimes can be the solution in and of itself. What if you attract the wrong kind of girlfriends or women, like I used to? What if we have no one to call because we lost our trust in other women through one too many painful experiences? Who can you go to after you entrusted something in confidence to a female coworker who betrayed you by broadcasting the information throughout your company?

In her book *Friendships Don't Just Happen!*[21], author Shasta Nelson says "Some of us point to unhealthy relationships as evidence that we don't need a group of close friends, believing drama and friendship are one and the same. And yet, for all our foibles and painful memories, here we are. Still wishing we had a wee bit more love and support in our lives."

Each of us has a story or two about a betrayal we suffered at the hands of another woman. It doesn't have to mean that we can't trust women anymore. It's time to change that. With The Women's Code, I learned that there actually was support available to me all along. There were trustworthy women at an arm's reach who would have jumped at the opportunity to support me if I hadn't pretended that everything was always okay.

THE WOMEN'S CODE BONUS GIFT:

To discover the Women's Code 7 Keys
of Support *you can go to this page*
TheWomensCode.com/7-Keys
and download The Women's Code 7 Keys to
Support for added ideas for asking for and
receiving better support.

Not all women have a lot of experience receiving true support. When someone offers you support, it's not a burden for them. It actually can be their pleasure. Nor do you have to return the "favor" equally. Simple appreciation is usually all that is needed to make the exchange of giving and receiving support complete.

Heart-centered support comes from a place of generosity and a desire to be of service to others. It's a free flowing exchange that uplifts the giver as well as the receiver, and benefits both.

THE WOMEN'S CODE TIP

In The Women's Code we use a simple tool to give each other support. Use these phrases generously:

I see you

I support you

I believe in you

COLLABORATION: THE THIRD PILLAR OF THE WOMEN'S CODE

I have always regarded myself
as the pillar of my life.

MERYL STREEP, *ACTRESS*

The third pillar of the Women's Code is Collaboration. Collaboration is about finding better ways to cooperate successfully with each other while we live, work, and play. Understanding the principles of what makes a successful collaboration enables us to improve virtually any area of our life.

So how do you form a good collaboration? Collaborations are built on trust, and trust takes confidence and courage. As we change the way we think and view the world, the world around us changes to match our new way of thinking.

When you collaborate with the understanding that your uniqueness is valuable and you have a solid place in this world, you realize that you are not alone. You leverage your talents to a greater sum than its parts. As one author friend says, "A good collaboration is half the work. And double the fun."

Now it is time to start forming amazing collaborations that will inspire you. Doing this is easier than you think. In fact, it is the natural and logical outcome of applying the principles of The Women's Code. When we know which ego-RHYTHM we are in we are aware of what we want and need, and when we have identified how and where to get support—the outcome is better collaborations and relationships.

Effective collaboration is liberating. The sum of each part is greater than the whole. Functioning families, teams, groups, and circles leverage off each other's strengths and can accomplish great things. Indeed, we are stronger together.

While explaining this concept at my Women's Code Live Events, I discuss how an engine works. There are so many parts needed to make it run smoothly. After a breakdown, imagine taking the engine apart to examine what is working and what is rusted, old, and needs repair. Even one tiny broken part can make the entire engine sputter or break down completely.

One may wonder which is the most important piece that holds the engine together? Is it the strongest one or the smallest screw? Perhaps it is the lubricant that makes running the engine even possible? Who is to say which part is the key component? The engine needs every single one.

Just like in this example, at life and at work we need each other so that our lives run better and we fit together just as perfectly. In good collaboration we acknowledge that each person has a function that is needed for the best outcome. In business we need creative people who have concepts, people who I call *maximizers* who know how to make the most out of ideas, and money people who can manage the in and out flows and balance budgets. In our life, we often choose people with a variety of attributes, there are our party friends, our cry on the shoulder friends, etc. It is not necessary that all people need to be equally good at everything. Each person does their part—knowing where to get the best deals, or how to fix things, or how to make us laugh.

The key to collaboration is to not assume what someone else is thinking, or why other people act the way they do, or why they are not good at all things. Rather, it is to encourage the different contributions to flow together for maximum collaboration and fun.

Remember the example of Melody? If we had known her story we would have had a better understanding of her situation. We may not have judged her based on her appearance. But we didn't know what was going on until she shared her story with us. My point is that *every* woman has a story to tell. Each of us has had her difficulties and with The Women's Code we learn how to appreciate our differences. Because when given the opportunity, most women I have met are truly beautiful inside.

It's also helpful to be aware that men and women process information differently. Just think about the difference between introverts and extroverts. In good a collaboration, we leave room for personalities and character differences. We are stronger together because of our differences. That is why we are collaborating in the first place. That is what empowerment is all about.

When it comes to collaborating, our differences benefit the collective effort. That is the heart and soul of collaborating. Instead of asking what does she have that I don't have, ask what does she know that I don't know? Once you incorporate this technique, you can use it to your advantage in all areas of your life. Believe me, part of our getting from overwhelmed to awesome is not having to do everything ourselves anymore! It is a big relief to know someone else can add to the picture.

For example, while my organizing skills as a former professional producer are exceptional, I chose to hire a project manager because I knew that Nancy was even better at it than I was. And the best part is that I am learning from her how to manage a team with multiple personalities. Not surprisingly she has had ideas that I wouldn't have been able to come up with.

Too many of us got caught defending our own way of life, our ideas, and our ideals and we ended up feeling isolated and misunderstood. We simply forgot to stop and take a moment to think, plot, or plan to see if there may be a better or easier way to accomplish our goals. Instead, we reacted. It's difficult to collaborate when we don't trust anyone else to do anything correctly.

A key point of Collaboration is not to backstab. Although we might not overtly and directly backstab other women, we may be around other women who do. There are ways to shut down backstabbing conversations without being annoying, a stick in the mud, losing friendships, or alienating yourself. Even if they are not in the room, it's important to support other women or at least to not throw them under the bus.

The following are some helpful ways to improve collaboration at the office.

When leading collaborations in the workplace, if the situation digresses, perhaps even gets a bit petty, do not take it personally.

You have a choice. You don't have to be reactive. Rather, you can simply guide the group to refocus on the common goal. Ask how do *we* get to our goal? Based on our individual strengths how can we *each* contribute to getting there?

A simple example where people get caught in losing the original objective is the professional network LinkedIn. I run two LinkedIn Groups and so many times I see how a participant gets caught in critiquing a comment where the original discussion has long been forgotten.

So, how do you lead an effective collaboration?

Here are a few key points to consider:

- Lead with compassion and kindness.
- Always assume the best intentions because it probably was meant that way.
- Understand that it might take a few meetings for the collaboration to "click."
- Mind your language and make sure that you are asking the right questions.
- It's better to ask what you need to do to support others rather than to assume.
- Be open to teaching and being taught.
- Start every day as a new day without yesterday's baggage.
- Make it about the people and the relationships.

The leadership style that I teach is called Leadership on C.U.E. It celebrates women's attributes and creates a leadership style that is natural to us: Compassion—Uniqueness—Empowerment. We exercise compassion for each other and what is important to us. We celebrate our Uniqueness for each has something different to contribute. We empower each other, for true power comes from within. That kind of empowerment allows us to step up to be leaders in our circles, because it means better teamwork and effective collaboration.

Another benefit of collaboration is that it builds our self-worth. It produces better results and makes us look smart and efficient. In every collaboration, we impart our knowledge to the group and in return we learn something new. Even today, it's such a relief to know that I don't have to be an expert in everything. Even when I say that to myself I can feel my shoulders relax. I take a breath. I don't have to do this on my own. I am not alone. I have a great team that I can trust to deliver excellent results. Sure, it takes time and trust to build a team and you may not find the right people to collaborate with right away but you'll get there. I promise.

The Women's Code promotes staying away from lunch cliques or other exclusive circles. It is so much more fun and engaging to be able to participate in a broad variety of circles. For example, if you are working in an office you could ask your colleagues from a different division to lunch with you or strike up a conversation rich with questions. That person might divulge a secret or two to success and make you the better for it. You never know, in the future you might just be the addition to their team that they have been looking for. Or you may want to bring them on to complete your team if that person adds a skill that you are missing.

In the collaborative process, we are both the student and the teacher. We impart our knowledge and others will teach us something new. It's okay not to be a "jack of all trades." Become an expert and shine in your niche and allow others the freedom to do the same. In business, when you recognize talent instead of being jealous of other team members, make an effort to learn from them. Befriend them. What do they know that you don't? You will expand your expertise and strengthen your collaborative efforts.

THE WOMEN'S CODE TIP

Always assume the best of everyone. We do the best we can with the information we have.

During a Leadership course at the Wizard Academy in Austin, Texas, the principle of collaboration was exceptionally demonstrated. One of the team exercises was to communicate to the group what each woman's strength was. Then they decided what job each should take on based on a fictitious assignment. One of the women, a strong extrovert with razor sharp smarts immediately took charge.

She declared that she would go first and suggested that a lady named Christine should go last. Why? Because Christine was an artistic and quiet introvert who first had to have time to think about what she wanted to say before she felt comfortable enough to state her preferences.

You may assume that the extrovert was faster and smarter to take charge so she could pick the best job for herself, leaving others who were not so aggressive to choose after her.

With The Women's Code awareness the extrovert took charge of the situation because that is her strength. She knew that the introverted Christine did not do well when put on the spot so she made sure that her team member had time to prepare herself for her turn. Christine, in return, was grateful for not having been put on the spot right away and given time to collect her thoughts. Each of the women brought 100% to the exercise. This is a fabulous example how understanding The Women's Code Pillars changed what could have been a frustrating situation riddled with misconceptions into a successful collaboration.

Now let's imagine how this scenario could have played out without the group following The Women's Code Pillar on collaboration. The extrovert takes charge and puts everyone on the spot right away—because that is what extroverts do. The other extroverts jump right in, not giving the introverts one moment to collect their thoughts and get a word in. The extroverts leave feeling exhilarated about a great meeting shaking their heads about how some people just have nothing to say. Whereas the introverts may say that this meeting was a waste of their time because nobody wanted to hear what they had to contribute! Have you experienced a meeting like this?

Remember that we always have a choice. We can either react based on our past experiences or assumptions. Or (and this is what The Women's Code is all about) we can dig deeper to find hidden nuggets of inspiration and wisdom. The world is not a conspiracy. The way we perceive what comes toward us simply reflects the level of clarity that we are operating from at the time. If we expect negativity that is what we will experience. Whereas when we change our mindset to a more collaborative one, we will begin to experience fabulous collaborations that we truly enjoy and benefit from.

Collaborating The Women's Code way is liberating. It's fun. It frees you up to have better friendships, and work better with people. When you collaborate, life is no longer a battlefield. It's a do-able, achievable, and fulfilling adventure.

THE WOMEN'S CODE BONUS GIFT:

To discover the Women's Code 7 Keys of Collaboration *you can go to this page TheWomensCode.com/7-Keys and download the 7 Keys for more ideas on how to improve collaboration.*

FIX YOUR LIFE—
SAVE YOUR SANITY

We have two choices: We lament about our lives and stay where we are or we push through our fears and make changes.

BEATE CHELETTE, *ENTREPRENEUR AND AUTHOR*

Finding the support we need through the principles of The Women's Code has been proven to change lives. It can change your life, too. Change is possible when we acknowledge the seeds of truth. When they fall on fertile ground, they take root. You may laugh (it's okay, I've been laughed at before) but I say this with absolute confidence The Women's Code can and will change the world if we are ready to shift our thinking.

My dream is that women everywhere will adapt the ideas and principles of The Women's Code and make it their own. In every country and in every language, it can and will change the way women feel about ourselves, interact with each other, lead, and communicate on all levels in our lives.

We need that shift to begin and along with new, practical tools and tactics we can fix our lives and save our sanity. Women are overwhelmed, unhappy, and disappointed. Women can't fit more into their lives because it is already bursting at the seams. And despite the thousands of things that we do every day, we never seem to be able to get ahead.

There is nothing wrong with women. What we need is a new baseline. The Women's Code welcomes, accepts, and respects every woman's choices rather than making us aspire to achieve impossible expectations.

This Women's Code movement is your first gentle nudge to join us. It is a hand on your shoulder. It's the voice that tells you that you can live the life that you really want, one ego-RHYTHM at a time. It's the support you've always craved. I personally have full confidence in you. I believe unswervingly in you. Some of us may have never heard those words before, which is why I'm saying them now. No matter how far behind the starting line you are, The Women's Code can help you turn things around.

The Women's Code is a new way of thinking, living and working. It is your lifeline. It has to feel right for *you*. It has to be right for *you*. And only *you* know which of the many tools, ideas, and principles introduced ring true for *you*. Start anywhere you want. Or follow the outline of the book. Begin by finding your ego-RHYTHM and discover your Main Focus. Use The Three Pillars to focus on getting your career together or dive into finding a better Work-Life Balance. You are empowered to make your own choices. The Women's Code is here to support you in them.

Truly the time is now. If we don't start to change and build our support networks with a more realistic baseline, I am afraid there will be dire consequences for women that will continue to compound. We are at a turning point because not only do we have record divorce rates, and record numbers of single moms but now a recent study from the National Academy of Sciences shows that life expectancy for some U.S. women is declining[22]. This does not surprise me. We added a second shift to our already busy schedule. We are unable to trust our girlfriends. We barely take the time to take care of ourselves. So, what else could the outcome possibly be?

You can begin today. Start with baby steps. Sometimes all you need is one idea to begin, one opportunity, or one person to believe in you. My Women's Code journey started with two women who believed in me. Carol and Kelly saw what I couldn't see in myself and never gave up on me. They showed me love and support through my darkest hours and accepted me for who I am. I finally received a glimpse of what it was like to have true support from women I could trust.

As a single mom, I was usually not invited to social events because most of them were for couples. But these two women were the exception. Kelly was the only married woman who would invite a single mom to her table and into her house for family functions, holidays, and intimate get-togethers. It didn't matter if I was the only single woman, Kelly made sure that I always felt welcome. Carol was my shoulder to cry on. My neighbor from across the pool, she opened her *"Midnight Cafe"* where I sat on her patio many nights often after midnight (hence the name) pouring my heart out to her, and sometimes her husband, when things kept going wrong. This fabulous married mother of two kept assuring me that I would come out on top. She was my daily pillar of sanity. Carol was a great listener and a true friend. To this day she invites me to family gatherings, birthdays and graduations. We've become an extended family for each other. The level of my gratitude can't be expressed adequately for either of them.

The Women's Code can transform your life, too, if you chose to allow it. I have witnessed hundreds of women go through the program and implement the Code in their personal and profession lives and achieve all levels of success, satisfaction, and happiness. We've put together our favorite case studies later in the book for you to peruse.

During our Live Events one scenario plays itself over and over again. Women at first are uncertain if it is safe to open up. Certainly, what happens in the room, stays in the room. But for some, we have mistrusted women for so long that it takes them a while to realize that this truly is a safe environment. It takes courage to open up.

But, women recognize quickly just how badly others have been hurt, too. Suddenly we relate and comfort each other. It's a privilege to be a part of this transformation, and the results for women are instant. It can get very emotional. This is what I call *experiencing the baseline*—when we know that we are connected on a fundamental level and we are really not that different from each other.

So take your time. Be gentle, authentic, and honest with yourself. It takes time to build meaningful relationships, especially when you have a little bit of undoing to do. Remember, this isn't about perfectionism as we're leaving unrealistic expectations far behind. The Women's Code doesn't guarantee that you'll never face adversity again. Rather it's a process to let go of the past and start rebuilding your relationships with women. I respect and honor you for even being willing to try. Recognize that as you change, you will attract a higher caliber of people around you and a richer experience in your life.

THE WOMEN'S CODE TIP

There is another side to every story. When we understand that each of us has a story, we realize we are all the same. That is when we can stop the critiquing and beating each other down and rather extend a helping hand toward each other without fear of retribution.

The ego-RHYTHM concept gives each woman the right to live her own life and focus on her own priorities as she moves through the different phases of her life. Each of these rhythms has its ups and downs and in each of them we may need a different type of support. The Women's Code teaches you how to identify what kind of support you need and how to ask for it in a way that is from a genuine heart space.

You've met a few thought leaders in this book before but there are many more trailblazers who are changing the way women interact with each other. We aren't buying into the same old clichés. It's clear to me that we are in a turning point in history.

Christine Bronstein created the organization A Band of Women. After the birth of her third child she had difficulty coping with postpartum depression. Sometimes pain is a source of inspiration. Very much like my own experiences, Christine discovered that other women had gone through this before and that there was a support network. Her coping and healing began through friendships with women that are so tight and deep that she affectionately started to call them "wives." She got the idea that other women were looking for the same connection and founded A Band of Women[23], a San Francisco based national organization dedicated to "A New Kind of Sisterhood" which helps women connect and support each other.

Another trailblazer to watch is Kathy Korman Frey from the Hot Mommas® Project[24], an "award-winning social venture that pairs the world's largest digital case study library of female role models with cutting-edge teaching tools." The result? Confidence and key success factor increases of up to 200 percent among women in Gen Y, Gen X, and beyond. They are sending the message loud and clear that it's okay to stand out and be successful. The Hot Mommas have your back when you want to figure out how others became successful.

Sheryl Sandberg's book, non-profit organization[25], and call to action "Lean In" for women who want to advance in corporations got a lot of attention just recently. Remember the Career ego-RHYTHM? That might just be the support you need when you want to get serious about corporate advancement!

Shasta Nelson's GirlFriendCircles.com[26] is teaching women how to be a girlfriend again to other women. Not everyone had positive examples of female friendships growing up. And for those of us who didn't, she shows us how, step-by-step. Can we ever have too many girlfriends?

I appreciate and love the women behind these projects and organizations, and of course there are many more. Bravo! Each of these organizations and initiatives are part of the same vibration of The Women's Code. Why? Because the Code is inclusive of all organizations and behaviors that elevate women to step into balance and power. We are in this together. Each of us has a unique piece of the puzzle and together we form one beautiful picture of support, liberation, and acceptance. We need each other.

If you can't find enough reasons to change for yourself, do it for your daughter. And if you don't have a daughter, do it for the next generation of women who need to trust women more so now than ever. The Women's Code gives us a platform and a roadmap to the breakthroughs we want to see in our lives. The time is now to build better relationships and realize that when more women achieve real Work-Life Balance and success everyone benefits, not just a select few. That's when we don't have to worry about "yellow roses" anymore.

As The Women's Code started working in my life, I began to get more excited. There was a smile on my face, sometimes for no specific reason. I just felt so good. I was having more fun. I no longer felt alone. I had a better social life. Wonderful company surrounded me. And today, I am HAPPY and that is what I wish for all of us.

To get The Women's Code working for you, identify the most pressing area of your life that needs the most attention. Then turn the page to learn how to experience a more fulfilling Work-Life Balance.

FINDING YOUR WORK-LIFE BALANCE

One thing is for sure: Women have a new kind
of power in the workplace, in the marketplace,
in the boardroom, and in the bedroom. Women
have as many definitions of power as there are
women to use it.

OPRAH, *MEDIA MAGNATE*

The problem is simple. Women's lives are out of balance because too often we put ourselves last. We are the last ones to take care of ourselves. We are the last ones to go to bed. We're the last ones to schedule time for ourselves away from the stress of work or children, but there is a way to bring our lives into balance.

Through my many interactions with women in The Women's Code, I often see women who are hopelessly overwhelmed and overworked. In a previous chapter, I shared Carol's story where she had put herself last, not even asking for some time out for a bubble bath!

This may seem like a small example but it points to a huge problem. I see women out of Work-Life Balance every day. It costs us more than we know. Our lives have become so busy, there is so much to deal with that we go on autopilot and just work, work until we collapse under the pressure. Sometimes we get sick or simply want out. After hitting our boiling point, we seek a divorce, turn to alcohol or pills, endanger our job, or just check out and feel like a robot, going through the motions.

I also meet many women, often in their early forties and above, who feel tremendous pressure to get a career going ... *now*. We made our families and our husbands a priority for two decades. We learned the hard way that the job market didn't exactly wait for us and we feel we don't have a minute to waste. We want to be financially independent. We want to define who we are and choose a career that makes us happy. Others are entrepreneurs and independent without a significant other (either by choice or from divorce) and the pressure is on. Big time. Single moms, by definition, do most of it on our own. Is any of this feeling familiar?

The women I described and whom you have met in this book all have one thing in common. Race, age, profession, background doesn't matter. We are **ALL** overwhelmed. And strangely enough we feel guilty for something that we can't quite explain. We lack confidence and we give ourselves very little credit for what we have done. Our achievements are all but forgotten, rather we speak about everything that we *haven't* mastered yet or have missed out on.

One of my coaching clients, an artist, compares this to feeling invisible. Let me explain. After feminism there were many women who pursued their careers above everything else. But not everybody went for the corner office. Some of us choose a more traditional path and focused on motherhood. Maria Shriver says "Having kids—the responsibility of rearing good, kind, ethical, responsible human beings—is the biggest job anyone can embark on."

For a decade or two, full time stay-at-home mothers support their children, husbands and often their husbands' careers. We were devoted to a home life. As our kids got older or left the house, we suffered from Empty Nest Syndrome. Now we feel invisible because we have no footprint outside of our immediate social circles. Without a career identity, we feel unimportant to society because we didn't make a difference in the world and therefore are "invisible."

Women at crossroads look at three hard choices. After twenty years many educated and well-trained women find ourselves without employment opportunities and are back at entry-level jobs, competing with twenty year olds for a retail position at The Gap. Or we give up any career plans and volunteer because we want to be involved and make a contribution somewhere. Paid or unpaid—it doesn't matter. Or thirdly, women in our 40s pursue, for the very first time, our dream of setting up our own shop and living out our passion. It can be very overwhelming when we've missed 20 years.

Even women who have always been in the workforce report feeling overwhelmed. One of my private coaching clients is a journalist and small business owner in the UK. She shudders at the thought of all the advanced technology that she is expected to understand and use so that she can keep up with the much younger competition. Technology alone advanced so monumentally that it can be a fulltime job and overwhelming just to stay competitive and sharp.

Another example comes from a different client who is building her business and is searching for the right business model. The sheer amount of choices can be overwhelming. When you do not have a minute to waste, the pressure is on not to make any unnecessary mistakes.

Sadly, this very feeling of being overwhelmed and the inability to find solutions fast enough translates into the very reason why some women lack confidence or worse—give up.

The Women's Code serves us in so many ways. When we discover our ego-RHYTHM and make a conscious choice about our Main Focus, we can take charge of our lives because we state clearly "This is what I am doing now." That is our start now button. It signals that it is time to rebuild our confidence from within. Because we have given ourselves permission to focus, for example, on motherhood for one rhythm, or to focus on our career for another rhythm, or our relationship. It's this ability to focus on one main thing at a time that saves our sanity. This is where the balance starts.

If we can't find a balance, we will see more signs of dissatisfaction showing up in all kinds of statistics. This particular one is very alarming. A new Gallup survey was reviewed by Forbes[27] and states that 71% of all employees are "not engaged" or "actively disengaged." In short, they don't like their jobs. How is that even possible and why? I shake my head and wonder once again how we got to such a discouraging place. We spend so much of our lives dedicated to work. What I have observed is that if we can't pinpoint what is missing from our lives, because we are internally not happy with ourselves, we often revert to blaming outside circumstances. And that usually is the relationship or the job. It is so much easier to lament about the job, complain that we are not appreciated, or that our boss is horrible. It releases us temporarily from having to make changes from within.

So how do you get from being overwhelmed by external circumstances to feeling awesome from within?

The first step is to get back to our baseline. Let's find our starting point, remember: *You Are Here*. In The Women's Code Live Events and in the Online Work-Life Balance Course, we get ourselves back to our baseline with a few easy steps.

The first step is so simple that you may not think it is necessary. But the day only has 24 hours so there is an actual time limit to what can be done. The key to a functioning balance begins with relearning what is possible within a 24 period.

Here was typical day when I was a single mom, struggling to raise my daughter with no outside help:

- 6 a.m. Get up. Get breakfast ready. Get Gina up and ready. Get myself ready. Get her out the door and in school by 8 a.m. (2 hours)

- Drive to and from work, 2 × 30 minutes (1 hour).

- Full day of meetings, strategic planning, conference calls, and more. No lunch break (9 hours)

- 5 p.m. Pick up my daughter. Go to grocery store or pick up dinner. Do errands. Home by 6.30 p.m. (1.5 hours).

- Supervise homework. Cook dinner ready by 7.30 p.m. (1 hour).

- Clean up. Watch TV. Playtime. Do load of laundry by 9 p.m. (1.5 hours).

- ✳ Get Gina ready for and in bed at 9.30 p.m. (30 minutes.)

- ✳ Check email. Quick chat with a friend. Catch the news. Be in bed by 11 p.m. (1.5 hours)

- ✳ Barely get 7 hours of sleep.

- ✳ Start all over again.

Looking at my schedule (and I'm sure yours is not too far off this one) when exactly was there time to work out, enjoy a bubble bath, have a social life, go for a walk with the dog, get our hair or nails done, date, spend quality time with our partners, advance our careers, have girls night out, go to the PTA meeting, learn another language, be the room parent, pick up a hobby, learn how to cook gourmet meals, and decorate our homes like Martha Stewart? Impossible.

THE WOMEN'S CODE TIP

The key to a successful Work-Life Balance is to devise a realistic plan and set priorities. We know our Main Focus. We have decided what is most important to us. That gets scheduled first.

But so few women see it that realistically. So many of us are still stuck trying to do it all, at once. And then we get so mad at ourselves when we can't.

THE WOMEN'S CODE BONUS GIFT:

I designed a (Life) Balance Plan and a Balance Training that will aid you with your weekly planning so you can start feeling good about all that you get done in a day. This is available to you at no cost. Simply go to this page WomensCode.com and follow the instructions.

In any case, let me show you the fundamentals on how to create a (Life) Balance Plan right now:

First Step: **(Life) Balance Plan**
In the (Life) Balance Plan, your first step is to write down how many hours a week you want to do things like: play with your children, spend quality time with your partner, go out, and even how many hours you want to sleep. Once you know how much time you want to allocate to the parts of your life that make you happy then you design your (Life) Balance Plan around those priority activities.

Second Step: **Remember your ego-RHYTHM**
The next step is remembering your ego-RHYTHM. There was simply too little or no time to have a busy social life when Gina was in elementary and middle school. Our children are always our priorities and we only have them in our daily care for a limited time. When Gina went to college and I entered my Me ego-RHYTHM,

for the first time in 18 years I could make it all about what I wanted. And I did. I've traveled, played, build my social circle, got involved—this rhythm was definitely about me time.

That is the beauty of ego-RHYTHM. When you move from one into another you can enjoy life so much more. That didn't mean I didn't miss my 'baby' after she left for college. I couldn't even go into her empty room for six months. But I knew I had experienced, and fully lived, my Mom ego-RHYTHM, so I had no regrets when I transitioned to my next ego-RHYTHM. That is what our experience will be when we follow the principles of The Women's Code. We will be able to finally live in the moment. The journey is the reward after all.

I have come to realize that happiness is in essence a choice that we can make with the right tools and mindset. Instead of being upset that we can't do things when we have children and then paradoxically being upset when they no longer need our attention—how about we enjoy both when the time is right? Happiness starts with living more in the present and creating more joy and balance in our daily lives. Choosing what we need to do by our Main Focus can create great happiness in our lives.

Third Step: Scheduling

And then, we schedule it. If it is in the calendar, it gets done. If your kid's hair appointment is in the calendar, yours should be, too. I will never forget when Angela at a Live Event grabbed me, showed me her hair and said, "Do you see this? I haven't been to the hairdresser in two years. But my kids go regularly." Angela is a business owner and mom of four. It hadn't occurred to her to add her own needs and wants to the family calendar. You don't have to come last. And if you are not ready to come first, at least make sure that you are taken care of as much as everyone else.

When we follow these simple steps and put our needs in the calendar, we are not overwhelmed and overworked anymore. We may be still busy, but it's a good busy because now there is a balance, which benefits us, our family, our career, and everyone we come in contact with. Your relationship with your partner may improve significantly. I see this happening all the time. Men love The Women's Code because it teaches women to be specific, compartmentalize, and to communicate their needs in a clear way that men understand.

Women got into the habit of endlessly giving and somehow just expected our families and children to know what we needed. If we expect them to figure out what we need, we may end up waiting for a very long time. Women have not been taught effective, simple communication about what we need but expect others to know this intuitively. We are either too shy or believe that we would be too demanding, bitchy, or unreasonable if we asked for what we need and want. Or we simply don't know how to ask.

Communicating our needs doesn't have to be difficult. Here is an example. When your partner knows that you are asking specifically for Tuesday and Thursday nights off (from 6 p.m. to 8 p.m.) and he has to take care of dinner so that you can work out he will be happy to do that. Just make sure you let him be the boss and don't interfere with his choices when he is in charge. Tangible items are easy to agree to. Concepts are difficult to fulfill. "I need two hours to go to the gym" is a tangible and specific request versus "if you only would do more so that I can work out" is too vague.

As for your family and fitting in your needs, if your 8 year-old tells you that he needs a haircut, why can't you tell you him that you need one too? And then you make that appointment for Saturday and add it to the (Life) Balance Plan. Easy!

This little tweak in voicing our requests more clearly will help us to relearn how to communicate better on all levels. This is not about having difficult conversations about big complicated things. By making simple, precise, non-emotional statements, little issues won't turn into big ones. This technique works wonders and creates so many benefits for us on many levels.

Our children benefit because their needs are scheduled into family calendars with things like playtime, going to the beach, taking a bike ride. They have a place in the (Life) Balance Plan just like the grown-ups. Important family time goes in there as well. Your children are okay with you not being there on Tuesday and Thursday nights because you will be there on Saturday when all of you will go for that family bike ride.

Other women will benefit because when we are happy with our lives and within ourselves we don't envy their lives. We don't want what they have because we are choosing what makes US happy. Happy women love their own lives and everyone in it.

And mostly, we will benefit. No longer will we merely react passively but we have a plan. And a better life is the result of our choices. There truly is enough for everyone and it starts with self-care and finding a good work-life balance.

If this chapter speaks to you, you may want to check out The Women's Code Work-Life Balance Course: This course includes

24/7 Access to Online Modules, a specialized Work-Life Balance Training. You will create your (Life) Balance Plan that you design yourself that will get you better balance beginning TODAY. You will also get one (Virtual) 90-minute LIVE Lunch with me where you will have an opportunity to get your specific question answered. For more info please visit this page: TheWomensCode.com/Work-Life-Balance

If you'd simply like to find out if your life is in or out of balance you can take the 3-minute balance test: TheWomensCode.com/Balancetest

LEAD ON C.U.E. — A NEW WAY TO LEAD FOR PROFESSIONAL SUCCESS

You are only as good as the team you surround yourself with.

DONNA KARAN, *FASHION DESIGNER*

Before we dive into this career chapter, I want to point out that when it comes to business I use language that is specific and focused, which may make this chapter appear more serious. Success in your career requires determination, discipline, and focus. As a business consultant, I work with many different individuals and companies helping them to implement proven techniques that facilitate business growth and improve leadership skills.

If you are not interested in career advancement at this time, you may want to still review the leadership attributes because they are universally applicable in any setting whether that is a church group, a PTA meeting, or the next charity fundraiser.

Lead on C.U.E. is a female leadership style I identified and created that I will discuss briefly in this chapter. While this is not a business book, (there will be a Women's Code career book where we will go into much more detail how to build a company and lead teams) I felt it was important to share a few key nuggets about how to make it to the top and stay there. This chapter is just a first glimpse into my professional toolbox.

Before you fully pursue your career, you must first take care of your most pressing needs like your children or mental and physical health. That way you will be 100% ready to focus on getting where you want to go professionally rather than feeling split into a million different pieces. Objective career decisions can be difficult to make when we are out of balance. We are prone to increased self-doubt which can too easily turn into self-sabotage, hindering us to get to the next level. We may find ourselves making negative statements like "The job market is very bad," or "Who would hire me?" or "Why would anyone book yoga lessons or hair appointments with me when there are already so many others out there that do I what I do?"

The Women's Code uses a methodical approach to build a solid base for our confidence to grow. To pursue our professional dreams, we need to feel strong and confident. Our professional dream could range from running our own business to leading a corporation.

I wish I could tell you that there is an "easy" button to it all. I haven't found one yet. But there is an "I can do it" button. Even for serial entrepreneurs or executive managers with a proven track record, setting up and running businesses is work. Business and career building requires razor sharp determination. That is why equal importance has to go toward building our support system of friends and family. We need the balance to make it work for the long term.

Please note that the ideas in this chapter aren't just a one-time exercise but a mindset we acquire and incorporate while moving forward. This mindset helps us find a balance between work and our personal life. It is the key to sustainable and healthy long-term success. Instead of rushing to the goal in the distance, we chose to make the path of getting "there" enjoyable every step of the way. I truly believe that this is one of the most important parts to a balanced life.

Building our support networks and circles step-by-step will help us get "there." Rather than just work, and spend more hours alone at the office we want to plan our days so that we can enjoy good company. When we plan our workouts, long walks with girlfriends, dinner parties, networking events, lunches with other successful women or men—we make sure along the way that we will be in balance and not by ourselves when we get to the top.

It's best to set small, achievable goals that you can easily reach or even surpass. If you set goals that are too big and unachievable, you set yourself up for failure. Remember we are first building confidence. My advice is to start small and grow. So instead of saying "I am going to the gym five times a week", it is better to say "I think I'll start with two days a week". If you go more than two times, you exceeded your goal. And bravo! Plan one network lunch or meeting a week. Then if you do more than that, again you have exceeded your goal and start to build up your "can do" confidence.

The Women's Code applies the Three Pillars of Awareness, Support, and Collaboration not just for personal Work-Life Balance but also in your career. The Pillars help you to clarify what your next steps should be. Are you ready to push your career forward? Do you have the support you need? Have you acquired the knowledge and skills to get to the next level? Who is a part of it? Who do you need to collaborate with to make this happen?

Not every woman wants a high-powered career or desires to be a Fortune 500 president. We may aspire to be a manager at the local retail store and be content with that, or we may dream about our own hair salon, coaching business, or teaching yoga or Pilates to private clients. First, we get clear on what we want then we devise a blueprint and go after it.

When you have identified that this is the right time to pursue your professional goals, get serious. Keep reading. This chapter might be your favorite yet.

With The Women's Code we can advance in a corporate setting or build our dream business because when we work with our ego-RHYTHMs, we know our Main Focus and balance our lives better. Work-Life Balance gives us the foundation we need to take our career to the next level.

Next, take a look at the new leadership style I developed based on the principles of The Women's Code. It is called Lead on C.U.E. and it's an entirely new way of thinking and acting while pursuing professional goals.

THE WOMEN'S CODE TIP

*Female leadership traits are different from
male ones because we think and feel differently.
It is easier to succeed if we can embrace who
we are rather than trying so darn hard to be
something we are not.*

Women are nurturers, we are the center of our families and we
bring valuable emotional and intuitive insights to our jobs. We
can't compete with men on a male level, nor should we try. This
doesn't mean we don't have any less value than men. Not at all. I'm
saying that women are at our best when we operate within our
natural state of being. We set our own course by using attributes
that play to our strengths. These attributes are: Compassion,
Uniqueness, and Empowerment, hence Lead on C.U.E.!

C Compassion: ego-RHYTHM teaches us that each woman
has her own rhythm that determines her Main Focus. We
flow from one rhythm into the next. As we flow and as our
Main Focus changes we show compassion for ourselves
and also for everyone else. We have a strong intuition. We
feel. We sense. We understand. We listen. We don't judge
another woman's position but we have compassion for her
choices based on the rhythm of her life.

U Uniqueness: Every woman possesses multiple layers that combine and create a unique individual. In The Women's Code, we subscribe to the Core Code of Conduct that respects the uniqueness of all women. Please go back to Chapter 6 if you want a quick reminder on what the Core Code is. We accept without judgment that another woman is not like us. She is unique, just as we are. It is time for us to embrace our differences and stand up for who we are as valuable individuals, each knowledgeable in our area of expertise. We're open to learning, embracing and accepting what others bring to complete the circle of female empowerment.

E Empowerment: The online Business Dictionary defines empowerment as "based on the idea that giving employees skills, resources, authority, opportunity, motivation, as well as holding them responsible and accountable for outcomes of their actions, will contribute to their competence and satisfaction." There are many career opportunities and paths to choose from. We can be or do anything we want. We always have a choice in how we act, therefore we can channel this innate power into empowerment by taking responsibility for what we do and how we do it. It's not about seeking power in order to rule over others, but rather to be accountable, conscious, and competent. This is a multi-dimensional process that helps women regain control over our lives. It fosters and supports our power so we can apply this power in measured and responsible ways in our lives, communities and circles.

Leading on C.U.E. is authentic. It invigorates us and the world because we lead in sync with our innate preferences based on a Core Code of Conduct strongly rooted in familiar key values. It is possible to maintain authority, respect, and command while nurturing other women when we follow this principle.

I developed the Lead on C.U.E. technique from my corporate managerial experience and through research. I learned that the way most women lead needed some serious improvement. I want to be clear, though, that there are great women leaders in all areas of politics and business. I am also certain that there are many outstanding local leaders who are exemplary in their communities who never reach national recognition. I applaud all of these women. But for the most part great women leaders are not the norm. Sadly, they are the exception.

Let me explain from my own experience in corporate America how unsupportive women can be toward other women, especially when we make something out of themselves. At 42, my life turned around. I went from a self-doubting, harried, overworked, single mom deep in debt to a self-made millionaire. My stock photography business sold to Corbis, a company privately held by Bill Gates. I breathed a huge sigh of relief. Finally, my worries were over. But just for a moment before a new reality hit me.

I followed the false assumption that if I made something out of myself and became successful that I would be liked and accepted by other women. What I wanted was simple enough. I wanted more camaraderie in my professional life and a circle of girlfriends in my personal life.

After the acquisition of my business, men were the first to congratulate me on my success. They were the ones sending me bottles of expensive champagne. I was accepted as a successful entrepreneur amongst the best and smartest men around. I had proved myself and there were no more tests to pass. Based on my merit, I was "in." Once you've earned a man's professional respect, you're not likely to lose it.

Women were an entirely different issue. My success definitely didn't help my popularity. I certainly didn't expect a party, but I didn't expect alienation either. I was distrusted. Women thought that I "must have done *something*" to have achieved this level of success other than just working hard for it. More than once I heard that I just wasn't "one of them" anymore. The minute your financial struggles are over, immediately you are moved into a different bracket, like it or not, and it's not always a positive experience.

During this time, I completely related to Kelly Valen when she wrote in *The Twisted Sisterhood*[28], a book that is a huge eye-opener regarding the state of affairs between women, "If you appear too confident, especially if you're attractive, successful, or wealthy, many respondents underscored that what we really want to see are some flaws, failures, and vulnerabilities before we'll feel comfortable with you; we don't like our women too pretty, smart, or perfect."

This meant that I was alone. In my social circles, I felt like I had to hide my success if I wanted to maintain my friendships. I was branded a "career woman" and I had to overcome the she-tyrant, man-hater, ruthless bitch stigma that comes with the territory.

Was there *any way* to win this? No wonder the Female Success Paradox is so evident today. What a disappointment, and a sobering discovery. First, we worry about whether or not we will we get to the top. Once we get there, we find out it is not a bed of roses and we have to defend our success.

But for men it's a different story. Leadership isn't new. Men have been groomed for generations to become leaders. It is expected that they grow up and lead. To make it into Executive Management, men were expected to have these three traits: Power, Strategy, and Persuasion. It's what I call a PSP Leadership Style. They want to become powerful. They strategize how to get there. They use their power of persuasion to enlist other men to help them advance to positions of prestige. To support them, men have an unwritten code that guides them in how to step into power, manage power, gain power, and then pass power on to their successor. Indeed, without a successor plan, there is no future in corporate America for even the best employee.

A successor plan is when we find a person on our team and groom him or her to take our job so that we can move up and take our boss's job. Successor planning is a standard topic in employee performance reviews for men in Executive Management positions. While it is entirely possible that this has changed since I left the corporate world, I dare say that for women this is the exception not the rule.

The Wall Street Journal[29] cites a McKinsey study and describes the following facts as discouraging, although 83% of mid-level women have a strong desire to move up to a higher level in their companies, their chances of landing a senior executive job are only 60% as compared to men.

There are many reasons why women in corporations don't advance in accordance to their desires. From childcare costs, to lifestyle choices, to not knowing what footsteps to follow, it is exponentially more difficult for women to find the right support and Work-Life Balance to be able to have a fulfilling professional life.

Once you find a good position you have to face the office bitches and the women who use their power to terrorize other women at work. There are many stories that demonstrate how women misuse their power at work and often deliberately seek out other women as their targets. Is it possible that achieving power has been misinterpreted and what power means to women needs to be redefined? I say yes. Power is often coupled with success, and success means more power, but it needs to be balanced otherwise it can turn into tyranny. A better term to use may be empowerment. Empowerment—rather than simply power—means that you are supported, prudent, confident, and practice temperance. A Happy Woman doesn't terrorize another woman or put her down. A Happy Woman creates a Happy World not just at home but also at work. When we find greater satisfaction in our own lives, our ability to communicate and collaborate with others greatly improves dramatically.

Women business owners face even more challenges. When I produced still photography in the middle of a six-month production season Work-Life Balance was often impossible. I had call times where I had to be at the job at 5 a.m. in remote locations like the middle of a desert. And I wouldn't be home until 10 p.m. that night. I was a single working mom. It was very expensive and stressful to constantly have to juggle between making the choice whether or not I paid my bills or was a good mother.

Below are some of my personal strategies and dos and don'ts in business. These ideas work whether or not you are leading or are part of a team. Even if you are a part-time freelancer, an employee, or if you volunteer locally, the tips from my professional toolbox can help you to improve your day-to-day satisfaction in your chosen profession

Beate's Lead on C U E
Professional Toolbox

Say YES to:

Opening a conversation with a genuine compliment. This disarms everybody and sets the tone of mutual appreciation and feeling good.

Listening first and asking questions. What do you want to achieve? Where do you see this going? Engage your co-workers and your team members to share what their greatest strengths are in your next meeting. Be willing to let something be done by someone else. It's okay to disagree at a later point but it is important to ensure your team contributions are heard. I don't believe that you can ever listen to too many ideas.

Going over the process, your expectations, and deliverables when assigning a task. Know how you work best. Remember my "helicopter brain?" Ensure that your style of leadership is understood and supported by your team.

Giving praise generously. Acknowledge the little things constantly. Always start with a positive and end with a positive. For example, you can say, "This was an excellent first draft; here is what I want you to do next. If the first draft was this good, I can't wait to see the second with the improvements."

Understanding the vision of your business, what you seek to achieve, how you want to service your customers. Then share that vision with your employees.

Focusing on people and your relationship with them. Make it about them and treat them with respect.

Being generous with praise and compliments. Even if they are about tiny accomplishments. Acknowledge a job well done. Praise and support are the best motivators.

Preparing more. Get clear in advance about what to get out of a situation. Knowing your must-haves and negotiables aid all negotiations. Use I-statements so the person on the other end doesn't get defensive. When someone feels attacked, they naturally defend themselves. It's normal, we all do it, but it creates a stalemate and stifles productivity. Flip what you say around so it comes from your point of view. For example, instead of saying you did this and I'm really mad about it, start from a neutral, even humble, place. "Maybe I didn't explain things clearly, but from now on I'd like you to do it as follows..."

Leading by a good example with respect, not fear. Be the person others can aspire to be. Success comes with responsibility and it is something that I personally take very seriously. If successful people don't demonstrate that it is worth it to get to this point, others may lose hope for a better life. As an empowered woman leader we want to show that working and achieving a better life is indeed better and worth the struggle to get here.

Asking what tools or changes your team needs to do their best work. For example, one of my team members likes to work in Google Docs. But I can't stand it. At first I found myself insisting they use my preferred cloud file exchange server. Finally, I realized that if this helps to get the job done faster, so be it. As long as I get a good end result, should I really care? Try to understand how a person's work process may differ from the rest of your team.

Setting personal boundaries. Under no circumstances should you bring your most intimate personal issues into work. This is not the place for personal information and there can be too much sharing. I have a very, very painful memory of a former friend who I hired as my right hand man who couldn't keep his mouth shut. He blurted something very embarrassing and very personal out across the table during an introduction lunch to my new boss. When in doubt, don't share it. Too much personal information at work is often what gets gossip started in the first place.

Say NO to:

Hogging information. Freely share what you know at work and be willing to share how-to information and mentor other women. You are in charge of determining what mentoring others might entail. A once-a-week lunch constitutes mentoring. It doesn't have to be a daily instance.

Participating in lunch cliques. Don't go and spend lunch with the same people at the same table day in and out. Lunch is a great way to network and connect with other women and men throughout your organization and your industry.

Gossiping. When asked for your opinion unless you know the facts from both sides this can pull you into the middle of a problem between two people that you have nothing to do with. If you must, walk away citing that you don't know enough about it.

Listening to or feeding rumors. When you unwillingly hear rumors your standard response can be: I find that very hard to believe. You can't get to this level/work at this company/be in this position behaving like that." Always give the benefit of the doubt. One bad rumor can destroy an entire career. Yours could be next.

Bullying. Stand up for what is right. Bullying and gossip only works if it finds a willing audience.

For more information on how to advance in your career, you can check out the Career Course where we cover many more strategies. And, if you are ready to take your career to the next level, the Career Course may be right for you: This course includes 24/7 Access to Online Modules, your personalized Career Blueprint that you design yourself to get your career back on track or start moving toward a more fulfilling career TODAY. You will also get one (Virtual) LIVE Lunch 90-minute with me where you will have the opportunity to get your specific career and business questions answered. Please click here to find out more. Please go to this page to find out more: TheWomensCode.com/Career-Course

HAPPY WOMAN
HAPPY WORLD

There are a million ways to be successful.
You only need to find one. Yours.

BEATE CHELETTE, *ENTREPRENEUR AND AUTHOR*

Before I end this book, I want to say that everything is right with you. You have done everything you were taught to do. And you have done it well. Now, you are ready for something more. Something better. Something that is going take you where you never dreamed you'd go.

You are here now. You are learning this now. The timing is perfect. Say goodbye to beating yourself up and feeling guilty. You can implement the principles and elements as they apply to you during the different rhythms of your life. At Live Events, I often remind my audience that they will remember what they need to remember when the time is right. The Women's Code is non-judgmental. You move forward at your own pace.

So, let's piece together why The Women's Code is your foolproof fix that takes you from overwhelmed to awesome.

Each of us has a story. We may have been hurt physically or abused verbally. Our past may be full of deep scars. Our career may be at a standstill and we may have been passed over for the last promotion. Some of us are just disillusioned. Others have given up and function only on autopilot. We may have been beaten down or been disappointed so many times that it is hard to get back up.

But that was then. And that's where then should be—in the past. This is now. Now is where we begin to recreate our lives so that they fit us better and make us happier.

This is how The Women's Code works: First we identify our ego-RHYTHM. If you have not done this already, do it now. That is the basis of the entire process and your first step. ego-RHYTHM is a time-based concept that shows you where in your journey you are right now.

The 9 ego-RHYTHMs are your starting point. They are the red dot on the map that says: *You Are Here*. When you use the graphic in the ego-RHYTHM chapter you can see how many different ego-RHYTHMs you already have successfully completed. Well done! Congratulate yourself on all that you have already accomplished. Certainly, you will continue to master more challenges and enjoy more good times as well. If you have done it once you surely can do it again. It also releases us from judging our past experiences. They were merely rhythms. It is not always going to be like this, this too shall pass.

The ego-RHYTHM that you are in determines your Main Focus. All decisions and choices that you are making are evaluated by asking that one very important question: Does this help or hurt my Main Focus?

Once we know what our ego-RHYTHM is we can set our Main Focus accordingly. This allows us to live in the present. We are now in control of our lives. We begin to make choices that are good for us by asking the right questions.

ego-RHYTHM teaches us that we are allowed to change and set a new Main Focus. We do not need to feel guilty about not doing everything at once any longer because there will be a time for everything. We can give other women the same freedom we give ourselves to move through the different rhythms of our lives. We acknowledge that other women can be in a different rhythm than we are and we respect their choices just as they respect ours.

To define what will create happiness in our lives, complete the Want-It-All List. What do we want? What makes us happy? Where do we want to go? Without knowing where we want to go, no path will get us there. But if we know where we want to go we can map out our direction. You may choose to design your Life or Career Blueprint (available through the Online Course and in Live Events.) We each have a unique direction that we can follow.

The Three Pillars—Awareness, Support, and Collaboration are our perpetual guidelines and the backbone of The Women's Code. They beg us to ask the right questions: What is going on right now? Am I supported, do I support others enough? How can we collaborate better? These questions are universally applicable for work and our personal lives.

The Core Code of Conduct of The Women's Code outlines and reminds us of a familiar and updated behavioral code. We treat all women like we want our daughters to be treated. Gossip, bullying, deceit, and distrust are a thing of the past.

The Women's Code shows us simple steps to implement this Core Code of Conduct in our day-to-day life whether at home, at the playground, or at the office.

Work-Life Balance is established by reminding ourselves that our important personal or self-care tasks should get the same attention as work or the people around us. We utilize the help of the (Life) Balance Plan to relearn how to schedule a balanced weekly calendar.

We Lead on C.U.E, with more compassion, appreciate each other's uniqueness, and become more empowered. The Women's Code will teach today's women how to be confident with their power, become good leaders, and then pass on our knowledge to the next generation.

The Women's Code isn't an instant remedy to end all conflict. There will always be conflict. We will always face adversity. Our daughters will also face adversity. Conflict is okay. It's how we deal with it that makes or breaks us. In the heat of the moment, women can now go back to the Code. It can be a mediator. It's can be that third party that promotes fairness, right action, and peace during times of conflict.

I agree with Kelly Valen, author of *The Twisted Sisterhood*, when she writes, "We may not be able to control which emotions envelop us, but we can certainly manipulate, suppress, and otherwise control how it all manifests in terms of our outward behaviors and the effect we have on others."

I truly believe that The Women's Code is the next phase after feminism. First, we broke down the doors to power. Then, we stepped into rooms we never imagined we could enter. Now, we learn how to become amazing girlfriends, mothers, partners, and leaders, loyal to our gender who support other women so we can truly have it all. With The Women's Code we are rebuilding our sisterhood from the ground up so that we all can achieve our goals.

THE WOMEN'S CODE TIP

Know and believe that when another woman is successful—she adds to your success, not takes away from it.

The Women's Code is liberating because it is so deeply rooted in what we already know and the tools and principles fit perfectly into our existing beliefs. We first embrace ourselves and then our sisterhood once again and finally we have a code, our own Women's Code.

The Women's Code seeds are planted, they work because they unlock what you already know but may have forgotten. You have an abundance of Free Bonus Gifts to choose from, supporting documents and additional training is available to you should you decide you want a little extra help or simply want to enjoy the company of like-minded women during a Live Event.

Your happiness begins with your choice to do something about where you are. I know that most of you live good lives, but if you are like the many women I have encountered in my professional career and through my personal circles you may admit like they did, like I had to—that while we are thinking our lives are good we were not feeling it. That there was this little something that was missing. A dormant underlying dissatisfaction. Our lives may look good on the outside but inside we are not exuberantly happy. Things were just okay but really we want them to be great.

The Women's Code helps you to uncover what that underlying dissatisfaction is and with the tools and principles you can do it step by step. In our success stories chapter you will meet a few women who have worked with The Women's Code, and you can read their stories and how it helped them find a better, happier place. Still living the same lives—just a little better. Not frazzled, not overwhelmed … in a word awesome.

Women are the soul of our planet. We are the forces that make the world run. When we will find a better balance we become happier within ourselves and our relationship with our partners, families, circles. Our work improves as a logical result. And productivity shoots through the roof.

> When we know where we are
> When we know what we want;
> When we know what kind of support we need;
> When we can ask for it;
> When we get it;
> When we live in balance;
> When we Lead on C.U.E.

We can be a Happy Woman living in a Happy World

Beate Chelette

THE WOMEN'S CODE SUCCESS STORIES

For specific examples of how The Women's Code improved real women's professional and personal lives make sure to read The Women's Code Case Studies below.

Andrea Reindl
Co-Founder of Smarter Voice

"Almost four years ago my world came to a grinding halt. I was expending more energy then I had. I overcommitted like every other mom in my neighborhood. My marriage had fallen apart. And I needed to get back to work. I also needed to find myself again. I had become so lost in a harried, disorganized life. I felt disconnected from my purpose.

Then I was introduced to Beate and The Women's Code. She taught the power of timing and women working together. Her concepts were universal but they applied to the specifics of my increasingly complex daily life. I related to her. Her struggles were my struggles. She found her way out and was teaching other women to do the same. Applying The Women's Code principles, I gained a healthier perspective. I redefined how to look after myself. I've actually learned how to care for me first. As a result, I take care of those around me much better. And best of all, I learned how to ask for help.

I now have relationships with the women in my life. I have a support system that I built intentionally with amazing women and men. Thank you! The Women's Code is truly committed to helping women be the best the can be."

Christine Bory
Photographer and graphic designer at Artis Formae
Creative Studio

"One year ago, I stumbled upon one of Beate Chelette's videos. I clicked. I didn't know then but I was in for the journey of my life.

After spending the past 20-years devoted to my family and household, I looked back on my achievements with mixed feelings. The first part of my life, I was blessed with luxury as a civil servant's wife in Luxembourg. I had a loving husband and four beautiful, healthy, intelligent, easy-going children. Still, I had an intense feeling of non-accomplishment. I felt a void. I craved recognition and independence. At an age where most other women are deep into a booming career, I felt that I had stood aside. And it made feel so guilty. I felt shameful about not having a voice in women's emancipation. More so, I felt amputated from part of my identity as a person. My French Catholic education had given me a clear definition of what my place in life should be. Yet, I suffocated inside. Feeling like I was nothing to the outside world sealed my confinement. I realized nobody listened to me because I had nothing to bring to the table. Nothing to be recognized for and I felt so isolated.

I acknowledged my failure in the most important part of my life: myself.

With a Masters degree in Art and training in Photography, Graphic design and Visual Culture I thought I had a chance a great job. But the world didn't seem to want me. That's when I sought out help and found The Women's Code.

Beate was so honest about her struggles and personal life, I felt like I could trust her. She talked about wanting more out of life, having it all but not all at the same time, building a life of one's own. Her words immediately echoed in me (as they still do, to this day). I felt vindicated. The Women's Code gave me the strong sense of identity that I had completely lost on all levels: as a woman, as an entrepreneur and as a spouse-mother-homemaker. Acknowledging the lack of balance in my life was a revelation. A blueprint for the future was all I wanted. I was riveted to my iPad watching the online Women's Code Ambassador Course.

Throughout the course I discovered that my feelings were legitimate. Most of all, Beate's positive thinking and supportive words helped me reverse the incredible guilt and negative spiral I had sunken into. I re-established myself as the positive, kind and creative person I used to be. I learned to trust my intuition. It was confirmed that I had the resources inside of me to claim my rightful space in society. Someone listened to me. Finally, I had a voice.

Bringing women together in a community of thought, experience, and goals is the strength of the Women's Code. What goes on in my life goes on in other women's lives. Men compete to have their place in the sun. But women run against each other to have their place in men's world. This divides women in our quest to have it all. We need to gather together on strong, common ground to build a world of our own, ruled by our own Code that works alongside with men and benefits the world. The Women's Code is a clear path for women to make their way in this world and brings peace to the hearts of everyone."

Christine Dow
Site Manager and Writer, Seattle

"Before I started The Women's Code, I was recently divorced and a single mom. I was hell-bent to reinvent myself and achieve all my personal and professional goals. Then I tried The Women's Code. My perfectionist demands on myself were gently questioned. I gained insights using the ego-RHYTHM assessment tool. This helped me explore the impact of past hurts and conflicts. I examined my professional aspirations through a lens that honored work-life balance.

As one who typically compartmentalizes my life, The Women's Code led me to a breakthrough by honoring and integrating all areas of my life. With respect, care, and gentle nudges, The Women's Code program put me on the path to unabashed self-nurturing. I now go to bed at a reasonable hour rather than tackle a few work emails. I schedule exercise and time to prepare healthy meals rather than skip the gym to make an early meeting and scarf a Subway sandwich for dinner. I'm learning to play the piano. My son and I play boards games in the evening rather than argue about turning off the video game. All the while, I'm a successful manager and writer for a high-profile technology policy website. I just got a raise and increased our budget to hire more staff. The website I work for earned high accolades from Forbes as one of the top 8 tech-policy websites. All these professional successes have come without sacrificing my most important goals: self-care and time with my son. I believe that this is due to the beauty of The Women's Code.

Alice Fredricks
Editor, Los Angeles

"When I attended The Women's Code conference in Los Angeles, my reason for attending was blatantly self-serving. I was there to network for possible writing jobs. Times were tough. A once flourishing career in print journalism had buckled in the face of the digital revolution. For the first time in my life, I didn't know what direction I should go in. And it was taking a long time to figure out. I told friends I was in a "transition" when they asked what I was working on. I was stuck. Yet, I couldn't admit it to anyone. I had too much pride."

At the conference, Beate spoke with incredible energy and passion about helping women—helping us in the room—become happier and more successful in our careers and personal relationships. One way was by collaborating and showing support for each other, she said. And by not criticizing other women for their ideas, their clothes, hairstyle, their weight, or whatever. No good comes from that. She was right. I made a mental note.

She said that each of us has a unique voice that is dying to be heard. I loved hearing that. Especially as she recounted her "Decade of Disaster." And there she was, years later, hugely successful and inspiring other women. I knew what it was like to hold it together. But when Beate started talking about transitions my interest was piqued. She described how perfectly normal it is to be in one transition as we flow in and out of life's many rhythms. They are cycles focused on finances, health, our families, motherhood maybe, spirituality and career. We were right where we were supposed to be. What relief! I could exhale. I hadn't lost my way. I was just exploring my options.

The real value of The Women's Code was not so much in asking the questions, but in reaching out and making a connection. I had become too isolated, and didn't realize it until I went to the conference and participated and connected with other women. I walked in thinking I knew it all. But I left with hope and reassurance that maybe I didn't have to paddle alone. Pretty huge when you think about it. And talk about networking–now I'm happily among the growing group of women everywhere who have experienced the power of The Women's Code.

Beate Chelette
Creator of The Women's Code

"In the last few months my relationship was deteriorating on many levels. I just couldn't commit on any level. Nevertheless after five years, we still had serious plans of moving in together and making our relationship a permanent one. I couldn't make peace with the thought and after one failed marriage I wanted to be sure on the second go around. I confided my fears to four of my girlfriends.

I had to admit that it felt like a cruel paradox that on one hand I created The Women's Code while at the same time I felt like my romantic life was in shambles. I put so much pressure on myself that my life had to be a shining example how the Code makes it all "perfect". But then I reminded myself that The Women's Code isn't about perfection. Perfection doesn't exist. Especially, in a single working mother's life like mine.

I certainly could use another look at my ego-RHYTHM to make sure I was in flow. I desperately wished that I was in my Love ego-RHYTHM. But I wasn't. Using the Pillars I knew I needed a better awareness and support so I turned to trusted girlfriends and advisors. With their loving support, I ended a long but unfulfilling relationship and moved on into the unknown."

These case studies show how each of the women including myself was able to identify which area of her life needed the most balance and attention. If you are ready to gently fix your life and save your sanity, read on how you can get involved with The Women's Code.

HOW TO GET
STARTED WITH THE
WOMEN'S CODE

As we are wrapping up this book there are a few things worth mentioning. Some of you will have gathered enough new information that will, along with the Free Bonus Gifts, get you started defining what you want and putting a plan in action to finding your unique path to happiness and personal transformation to success. Let The Women's Code be your foolproof fix to take you from overwhelmed to awesome whatever that might be for you.

I want to personally thank you for allowing me to share my journey and my ideas about how women can collaborate with other women on an entirely new level. The seeds of The Women's Code have now been planted.

For some of us this is only the first step. Make the decision today to stop the nagging underlying dissatisfaction that we can and will eradicate for good. If you are ready I encourage you to commit to do what it takes to take control of your life, by getting in the drivers seat with a proven plan in place.

It is go time.

Our own surveys show that graduates of our programs say that the quality of their relationships with other women *as well as men* increase by an astonishing 65%. When you know what you want, are able to communicate it clearly, and know what makes you happy—the sky is the limit. That is my wish for you and I hope you are ready for it.

As an entrepreneur, coach, and speaker I can show you how to create your own personal Women's Code through my courses, live events and programs.

Are you inspired? Do you feel ready to take the next step? Do you want to learn more and become a part of The Women's Code movement that is sweeping the globe?

If you answered yes, consider any one of the following opportunities by selecting one of our three **online programs:** the Work-Life Balance Course, the Career Course or the Ambassador Course.

Work-Life Balance Course
(TheWomensCode.com/Work-Life-Balance)
This course includes 24/7 access to online modules, plus you will receive specialized Work-Life Balance Training showing you how to create your (Life) Balance Plan for better balance beginning today. This course includes one (virtual) 90-minute LIVE coaching session with me.

If you have a business and want to find out how to implement the ideas of Awareness, Support and Collaboration into your teams for better teamwork and productivity, and as a result a better bottom line, my practical and hands on tips will help you build your business, increase your revenues and get you back in balance so you can create the life you always wanted. If business and career is on your mind this course might be your perfect fit.

Career Course
(TheWomensCode.com/Career-Course)
This course includes 24/7 access to online modules. You get to identify your best skills and which ones you are still lacking to get where you want to go. This course will help you figure out how to get your career started, moving forward or back on track. I will guide you in designing your Career Blueprint. This course includes one (virtual) 90-minute LIVE coaching session with me where you will have the opportunity to get your specific career and business questions answered.

If you are a woman who wants to address both, your Career and your Work-Life Balance, I recommend our most popular Ambassador Course. This course includes all modules from the Work-Life Balance and Career Courses, plus additional modules.

Ambassador Course
(TheWomensCode.com/Ambassador-Course)
This course includes 24/7 access to all online modules. On the career side you get to identify your best skills, and which ones you are still lacking to get where you want to go. This course will help you figure out how to get your career started, moving forward or back on track. I will guide you in designing your Career Blueprint. On the Work-Life Balance side you will receive specialized training which will show you how to create your (Life) Balance Plan for better balance beginning today. There are additional modules on support and a break-through exercise designed to help you to break with old patterns. You will also get two 90-minute (Virtual) LIVE coaching sessions with me where you will have the

opportunity to get your specific career and business and work-life balance questions answered.

If you feel that you are the type of person who would enjoy the company and camaraderie of other women during **The Women's Code Live Events, Seminars and Trainings,** please go to the TheWomensCode.com/live to find out where and when we will be live in your neighborhood.

Please visit BeateChelette.com to book Beate to speak at your next event or to find out about our corporate training programs.

We want to hear from you. Here is how you can interact with other women through The Women's Code and participate in our movement:

Please share your experience on our Facebook page, Facebook.com/WomensCode.

To tweet us or follow our inspirations you can also find us at Twitter.com/BeateChelette.

If you prefer to watch video please visit our YouTube channel at YouTube.com/BeateChelette.

If you are looking for better networking and business connections with other women subscribing to The Women's Code please join our LinkedIn Group: The Women's Code.

For anything else please write to us at office@BeateChelette.com.

NOTES

1. Luscombe, Belinda. "Workplace Salaries: At Last, Women on Top." *Times*, 2010. Web.
2. *The State of Young America*. New York: Dēmos and Young Invincibles, 2011. Web
3. "The Third Billion | Booz & Company." *The Third Billion | Booz & Company*. Web.
4. "The Shriver Report." *The Shriver Report*. Web
5. Bryan, Meredith. "The Pink Ceiling." *Marie Claire*. 12 Dec. 2008. Web
6. "CareerBuilder." *CareerBuilder*. 29 Aug. 12. Web.
7. Namie, Dr. Gary. *Work Doctor RSS*. Web.
8. Namie, Dr. Gary. *Workplace Bullying Institute RSS*. Web
9. Snowdon, Graham. "Women Still Face a Glass Ceiling." *The Guardian*. Guardian News and Media, 20 Feb. 2011.
10. Chesler, Phyllis. Woman's Inhumanity to Woman. New York: Thunder's Mouth/Nation, 2009. Print. With a new Intro by Chicago Review Press.
11. "Stevenson, Betsey, and Justin Wolfers. "The Paradox of Declining Female Happiness." *NBER*. , 2009. Web.
12. "Mothers by Numbers." *Infoplease*. Census Bureau, Web.
13. Sandberg, Sheryl, and Nell Scovell. *Lean In: Women, Work, and the Will to Lead*. New York: Alfred A. Knopf, 2013. Print.
14. Frankel, Lois P. *Nice Girls Don't Get the Corner Office: 101 Unconscious Mistakes Women Make That Sabotage Their Careers*. New York: Warner Business, 2004. Print.
15. ego-RHYTHM is a registered trademark of Chelette Enterprises, Inc.
16. Maresca, Racel. "Drew Barrymore: 'I Don't Think' Women Can Have It All." *NY Daily News*. 6 Apr. 2013. Web.
17. *Mind Movies*. Web.
18. Taylor, Shelley E., Laura Cousino Klein, Brian P. Lewis, Reagan A. Gruenewald, Tara L. Gruenewald, Reagan A. R. Gurung, and John R. Updegraff. "Biobehavioral Responses to Stress in Females"
19. *Biobehavioral Responses to Stress... Preview & Related Info*. UCLA, 2000.
20. Berkowitz, Gale. "UCLA Study On Friendship Among Women—Health & Wellness—Sott.net." *Robotics.usc.edu*. UCLA,
21. Nelson, Shasta. *Friendships Don't Just Happen!: The Guide to Creating a Meaningful Circle of Girlfriends*. New York: Turner, 2013. Print.
22. Kindig, D., and E. Cheng. "Health Affairs." *Even As Mortality Fell In Most US Counties, Female Mortality Nonetheless Rose In 42.8 Percent Of Counties From 1992 To 2006*. University of Wisconsin, Web.
23. Bronstein, Christine. "A Band of Women." *A Band of Women*. Web.
24. Korman Frey, Kathy. "The Hot Mommas Project." *The Hot Mommas Project*. Web.
25. Sandberg, Sheryl. "Lean In." *Lean In*. 2013. Web.

26. *GirlFriendCircles: Introducing Women. Inspiring Friendship.* Web.
27. Gallo, Carmine. "70 Percent Of Your Employees Hate Their Jobs." *Forbes.* Forbes Magazine, 11 Nov. 2011. Web.
28. Valen, Kelly. *The Twisted Sisterhood: Unraveling the Dark Legacy of Female Friendships.* New York: Ballantine, 2010. Print.
29. Shellenbarger, Sue. "Why Women Rarely Leave Middle Management." *The Juggle RSS.* The Wall Street Journal, 11 Apr. 2011. Web.

CPSIA information can be obtained at www.ICGtesting.com
Printed in the USA
BVOW03s1656150414

350366BV00001B/1/P